SYNERGY AND COMMONALITY
The Key to Success

EVANS KWESI MENSAH

© 2019 Evans Kwesi Mensah

All Rights Reserved.

No part of this publication may be reproduced, stored in a retrieval system, or transmitted, in any form or by any means, electronic, mechanical, photocopying, recording, or otherwise, without the written permission of the author.

ISBN 13: 978-1-7325517-2-5

Contents

Author's Note	....	v
Dedication	....	vii
Chapter 1	Character..	1
Chapter 2	What Kind of Root System Do You Have?...........	5
Chapter 3	Learn and Know Yourself	7
Chapter 4	Fetal Formation Process and Its Implications	15
Chapter 5	Time for Everything...............................	19
Chapter 6	Be the Best at What You Do— Success Has No Particular Path (Part 1)	25
Chapter 7	Be the Best at What You Do—Success Has No Particular Path (Part 2)	35
Chapter 8	From Riches to Rags...............................	43
Chapter 9	Know Who You Surrounding Yourself With..........	49
Chapter 10	Do Not Eat Your Seeds—Plant Them	61
Chapter 11	Learning to Be Content with What You Have	65
Chapter 12	Diverse Talents	71
Chapter 13	Wastes in Life and in Business, and Second Chances...	77
Chapter 14	Good Leadership	83
Chapter 15	Guarding Against the Tongue......................	89

Chapter 16	Reaching Your Potential	93
Chapter 17	Some Victors Over Personal Challenges	103
Chapter 18	A Sense of Commonality	113
Chapter 19	Research on Case Studies Regarding Commonality	119
Chapter 20	Effective Listening and Its Impact on Commonality	131
Chapter 21	Some Uniquely Identified Ways to Find Commonality	137
Chapter 22	How to Use the Power of Commonality Positively	145
Chapter 23	Creating and Attracting a Sense of Commonality	151
Chapter 24	Perception or Ignorance?	155
Chapter 25	Mentors Versus Advisors	159
Chapter 26	Free Brand Promotions	167
Chapter 27	One Body, Many Parts: A Metaphor for Life	169
Chapter 28	The Dangers of Ignoring Cultural Differences	173
Chapter 29	Different Types of Relationships	177
Chapter 30	Followers	181
Chapter 31	My Invitation to the Martin Luther King Jr. Celebration By the White House	189
Chapter 32	The Fruit of Etiquette and Managing Incidental Situations	191
Chapter 33	How Leaders Find Camaraderie Despite Differences	193
Chapter 34	Recipe for a Perfect Taste	199
Chapter 35	Friends, Foes, History, and Commonality	203
Appendix	The Seven Main Wastes in Business	211
About the Author - Evans Kwesi Mensah		215

Author's Note

If you seek practical wisdom in this modern world, this is the book for you. If you are at a crossroads and do not know what to do, this is the book for you. If you need an inspiration of any sort, this is the right book for you. If you need reassurance to add value to your life and make a difference, this is the book for you. Also, if you're doing very well in life, but not sure of what tomorrow brings, this is a perfect book for you as well. Finally, it is for those who spend their lifetime blaming others for their failures rather than taking a second look in their own personal lives as an opportunity to add value to themselves.

I have carefully crafted messages covering every major situation in life regardless of your background, belief, culture, social class, faith and or origin. Strategies suggested were carefully designed and tailored on how to avoid the common "silly" mistakes that have led many people into tumultuous financial woes that jeopardize the rest of their lives. As well, those who have already fallen into the doldrums need this book to be guided out of the dire results of their mistakes. Call this book "Moses" then, for it is here to lead you out of your slavery

Far from being a mere rhetorical message addressed from a podium raised above the ground, with the people being lectured looking up, this book is on the ground. It is practically leveled with everybody in terms of its down-to-earth realistic solutions inspired by actual experiences and handy observations.

The environment I was exposed to, and the people that surround me at the time, and how things were seen, and my eventual self-realizations constitute the fulcrum of this narration. This makes it the more realistic, hence applicable to you too.

It took more than eight years to analyze and complete this inspiring masterpiece. This is just to suggest how meticulous and careful it took me with the entire process for the purpose of landing well. Each chapter is, therefore, a manifest combination of experiences that are uniquely inspired.

Having traveled quite a bit and seen a lot of things, I wrote this book on purpose to capture the mind of the reader and take you through a special and unforgettable journey. It is to affirm or contradict how you think. It is geared towards challenging and possibly influencing your mindset in a positive way. It is out to align your way of thinking. It is here to shoot your brains to a different level. I strongly believe that your life and relationship with people might be affected in a constructive way after reading this book— not to mention the fast-changing world, how it is ripping people off of many opportunities, and the suggested best ways to stay afloat. For instance, how do you give your best out only upon being granted the necessary security?

Have you identified what it is, that is driving your vision if you have one in the first place? What are your "aha" moments? Life happens but once, and when you miss out on important steps in life, it might cost you your life, your dignity, and probably everything you might have worked for or longed to possess. This book is dedicated to helping you be proactive, to sail above the waters in spite of life's turbulence rather than reacting to issues that might be avoided. It is also positioned strategically to help those who are yet to make major decisions, to be aware of the common pitfalls to avoid. Finally, it focuses on a blend of experiences in different cultures and how people create synergies and commonalities to associate with other people successfully. None of the above can be effectively successful if one does not have the right character and integrity to back it. This book, therefore, has been crafted to help with all of this and hopes you will have an open mind to learn and add value to your life.

Dedication

I strongly dedicate this book and appreciate the Almighty God for giving me life, the wisdom, strength and the ability to conquer this project with ease. All praises to you! I also thank my dearest wife, whom I call 'Baake', my rock, my critic and a selfless woman that I am blessed to have, who was my greatest support from the beginning, to write this book in the first place. This lady pushes me to the limits to achieve more. I am grateful to you. And to my lovely and talented children, Evans Jr. a.k.a. SJ, Ethan and Eamonn. These boys prayed with me literally and gave me the space and peace to write this book at ease. You guys are awesome and will grow to appreciate life even better. My siblings, Richard, William, Michella and Enoch, who all supported me, not just verbally but in all forms, even at a time dedicating in helping edit and paraphrase a few areas to make the reading and meaning of this masterpiece simple. I owe it to you. Many of my friends and close relations whom I cannot start mentioning names to omit anyone, you know yourselves, but Harry in particular, who decided to wear his 'Chicago Tribune' editorial hat when he was a young intern, helped in making sure every content in this book is in-line, in spite of his busy schedule working for a major bank on Wall Street, you're the best.

May this not be misconstrued, but I also want to thank every person who made life difficult for me at some point in life, be it professionally or on the street, you were the reason I became a better person, and so, though the roads might be rough at some point, it is all for a reason. You subliminally contributed hugely to the success of this piece. I have become toughened, more poised, more determined and more blessed as a result. My gratitude also goes to all of my mentors, coaches, mentee's, those who work with me professionally and on a voluntary basis, my silent supporters and everyone who one way or the other came into my life and made a positive impact. Everyone who took the time to conduct a survey or attended my coaching sessions on this, how can I thank you? Above all, except to the Almighty and my wife, my humblest gratitude goes to my parents Rev & Rev Mrs. Anyagli – Mensah (Dade), who are now in blessed memory, who instilled discipline, respect, provided education, clothing, shelter, food and all the basic needs for my siblings and I to succeed in life. They did everything as parents for us, even if it was at the peril and sacrifice of their personal dignity to create a better world for us. Thank you so very much. I apologize to anyone I might have missed, but you know yourselves. Thank you!

CHAPTER 1

Character

I was driving in one of the major cities of the United States quite recently when I got attracted to a very unique message displayed on one of the electronic signs attached to an old church building. It stated; "Character is how you treat people who can't do anything for you." I had to read the message quickly, as I was in moving traffic. The only reason it resonated with me was how true it sounded to me.

Using camaraderie to attain a certain level of friendship, which may or may not build a business relationship depends on the seriousness both of you attach to the relationship and how you gel. Possessing the right character is a great influential asset. Cultivate the right character and be consistent with your cultured behavior regardless of the outcome

Usually, and almost accepted as if naturally, we are very much ready to stretch our sinews to do anything even beyond our means for people in high, influential positions. Of course, it is mostly in expectation of immediate gain. Therefore, what happens when suddenly, the person or persons are no longer in that position? Our focus simply changes and we adjust to the next personality that occupies the same position. That is our attitude even towards people whom we may have needed. What of those from whom we expect no gain? Would they always matter to us? Let's face it, there is nothing wrong in helping people who may do something for you in return or who are doing something for you, but the irony of it all makes the message too true to be ignored. Try getting down from your 'horse' and see the number of Christmas cards you would receive, compared to the previous year when all was well with you. Sometimes, you need character, not prayer, to get you to the next chapter of your life's ladder. This is because no matter how hard we pray, character has its place and role. This is the strong truth lots of people fail to understand. While prayer is worthy, that isn't the answer to everything. Sometimes people pray and hope for miracles to happen in their lives, whereas all they need is character and the right attitude to attain it. If you lack a good relationship with people, you may succeed for a while but may hardly be blessed the way you may deserve it to the fullest. Learn to treat people with courtesy and respect because you don't know who would be used to bless you, even if not necessarily today, tomorrow. Sometimes that blessing is meant for someone else but through you.

The point is, when used properly, prayer can inform your attitude and can help you become more introspective and shape your character. To succeed you must not simply focus on prayer but on your attitude and character.

Consider a few instances in the Bible where it took ordinary people to save the lives of others:

Naaman who was recorded as one of the richest men in his time, and was very respected, suffered a disgraceful and contagious disease called leprosy. People usually become an outcast as a result of this sickness. Naaman, despite his wealth, had this. Before he got healed, it was his maidservant who suggested where her boss could receive healing. Considering Naaman's wealth and how he was regarded in society, he must have visited and invited some of the best doctors at the time to come over to cure him, but nothing worked. Who would have ever thought that the solution to his problem was in the mouth of his maidservant? Sometimes, the solutions of our problems are trapped in the mouths of people whom we might deem "not so important," or people in today's age who cannot easily be found in any search engine. The problem is, many are not humble enough to realize and acknowledge this. No wonder it is said, 'they have eyes but cannot see.

Remember also the Shunammite woman? This was a woman who had been praying for a child all through her life, I'm sure, but wasn't able to conceive. Like Naaman, she was indeed a prominent person and surely possessed wealth, but that wealth couldn't buy a child for her, at least not at that time. Do you know what finally broke the lid and paved the way for her to have a child? She had to take care of Elisha, who served as God's prophet. It was recorded that she honored Elisha and was very hospitable. She was kind-hearted, had the right attitude and character that came with it. It was not recorded this woman did all of that in anticipation of getting a child; she was just herself and doing what she was good at. Elisha, on the other hand, was used by God to speak into her life and into her womb. Guess what? The next year, she had a child. Sometimes all one needs to do is to be persistent and never waiver from doing good. That too is character! This Shunammite woman was gracious. Assuming she was rude and inhospitable, unappreciative, nor kind, she would still have been praying, fasting, 'binding', 'casting', and "breaking" the demons that are powerless anyway. A lot of people are going through similar situations right now. What they need to do is change course and do something right. Why not advocate for the destitute, fight the cause for the weak, or just feed the hungry? Try something different in addition and see the result.

FOOD FOR THOUGHT:

Sometimes, we are our own enemies. Our attitudes are our destiny killers. Some of you might have been rude to people that might have been divinely positioned to help you, but lost it. Some were angels in disguise, but because they didn't look as such or dress in that form, we despised them. Some may be keeping malice's with their destiny helper, but do not know. Some may be suffering from achieving something unique, not because they lack talent, but because they lack the right character. Talent is attractive, but I want you to know everyone can be talented, but character is a proof of discipline, and a proof of responsibility. Character sustains the attraction talent gives you. Character is virtue, and sometimes what we call favor is triggered by virtue. In all your aspirations, desire also for character, the right attitude, respect of people, and treat them right. Treat strangers with courtesy, and do not look down on anyone, or else you may expose yourself while looking down anyways. Be kind (I mean 'kind') and leave a positive mark. Your angel won't always be a winged one; anyone can change your life at any point in time.

The simple point is, prayer is not all. Build relationships and make sure they are positive, pure and relatable. Also, create a sense of commonality in those groups to enable others to also see what you see. It must be noted, however, that not all relationships must be kept; only some stick. Know the difference. Respect people, get character, and excel. Sometimes, you can do all of the above in the right way but may not see results the way you want them. My advice is, keep doing good, do not relent, and know that it is better to be on the right side of life as a matter of principle than be on the wrong side. Sometimes, the results are not meant for you, so just continue on the right path, for we live in a very puzzling, interconnected world.

"Whether right or wrong, it is my belief that Christian colleges place their emphasis not on that which divides us, but on the substance that binds us together. That commonality is the gospel of Jesus Christ. He commanded us to love one another—to set aside our differences and to care for "the least of these" among us. It is our unity, not our diversity, that deserves our allegiance."

- James C. Dobson, Life on the Edge:
The Next Generation's Guide to a Meaningful Future.

CHAPTER 2

What Kind of Root System Do You Have?

The Sequoia redwood trees, mostly located in California (USA), are some of the biggest trees the world has seen. One such tree in particular, named General Sherman, is in fact noted as the largest known living single stem tree on earth! It is 275 feet tall, 25 feet in diameter, and is approximately 2,500 years old.

Something that tall and huge is expected to have an incredible root system that goes deep down in order to stand that tall, right? Sorry to disappoint you, but, that is not the case with this tree. The Sequoia redwood trees have a unique root system that is a marvel, compared to their mammoth size. Their roots are relatively shallow. There is no taproot to anchor them deep into the earth. The roots actually only go down 6 to 12 feet, which is not that deep for such a height of a tree, yet these trees rarely tip over. They are able to withstand storms, strong winds, earthquakes, fires, and prolonged flooding. How can something up to 500 tons, reaching over 27 feet in height, and existing for many centuries remain standing with roots only going down about 10 feet? The secret about the redwood tree is that its root system is intertwined with the other redwood trees, more or less creating solid connections, thereby literally holding each other up. The trees grow very close together and are dependent on each other for nutrients, as well. Only redwoods have the strength and ability to support other redwoods. So, beneath the surface of these humongous, tall, statuesque trees are roots like the military who have their arms interlocked, standing and supporting each other so not to fall. They are preventing the adversaries of life from knocking each other down. They are also making sure there are plenty of nutrients to sustain growth.

This is like, original IOT - the Internet of Trees. They had created the Wood (tree) Wide Web long before humans found the World Wide Web. Most of the findings by humans are sprung from nature that already existed and are only now being discovered. We are late. We need each other to survive and succeed in life. Let us learn a lesson from this unique tree. Avoid backbiting, stop acting larger than life, stop acting like the world revolves around a person, eliminate jealousy, stop rejoicing when our perceived enemy is down, and genuinely care for one another for synergy and corporate success.

Synergy says $1 + 1 = 5$, not 2, and look at its compound effects thereafter. Imagine effects if the redwood tree parasitic or selfish traits. its very strength becomes a crippling weakness that could, in time destroy the whole redwood forest.

Consider also the climbing lianas, which are rooted deep in the soil and the ground, however, always needs the help of other trees to get to the top. If trees are not available, these lianas will find anything taller and well-structured to provide the support needed for it to climb up high. Sometimes lianas become taller than their support. Cut the support system, though, and the liana is almost useless because it definitely could not get to where it wants to without the support systems.

Can you imagine being a liana, seeing everyone under you as worthless and not important, feeling so high and on top of the world that you almost forget it was by taking on so many support systems that you have gotten to where you are now? Imagine it. If everyone that is supporting you who enable you to see the light decides to let go of you, where would you be?

FOOD FOR THOUGHT:

Just as the climbing lianas and the redwood trees rely on one another's support systems to succeed, one cannot do without others. We need a system of reliability and commonality with one another because what may work for someone may not work for you. However, this is not a license to be a 'jerk'. Avoiding people should not be a license to hate them, and always bear in mind, you do not know who might be opening the next door for you.

CHAPTER 3

Learn and Know Yourself

One common pitfall for a lot of people is the desire to be liked by someone else. This is not in any way a suggestion that you should not admire celebrities or people in authority, or wish to be a better picture of someone you admire. The point simply is to be yourself, your best self. The day you transform yourself to be like someone else, that might be the day you miss the biggest opportunity in life - knowing who you are and discovering your potential is key. That may be when someone may be looking for exactly what you had changed from. The wise have observed that, in this life, we are all writing an examination in one hall. Though we are in one hall, we are answering different questions from different examination papers, so those who strain to copy others are only gearing for failure.

You're a unique person and wonderfully made. Be known by who you are by making a name for yourself, and don't try to be like anyone else. Learn from others but remember they are unique, and so are you. It is good to have a vision and to aspire to be on top, it is not bad to aspire to be like someone, but it is always good to remain who you are but a better you. One cannot deny the fact that aiming at a goal propels you to do better. It is one thing wishing to be like someone in terms of personality and another to be like someone professionally. The latter may be better than the former, but even then, be your unique person at all times.

I am known to possess a signature smile most of the time; people often refer to it as contagious. I have received many compliments for the way I carry myself and continue smiling no matter the circumstances, but I have also been judged by this same signature smile of mine. When I was in the corporate world, some people connote it to mean weakness because it was believed that, when you're too nice, you would find it difficult to control other people while in a high position. I vehemently disagree.

I was tempted to change my attitude just to please others, but the more I tried, the worse I became because that wasn't me. There is always a challenge out there that is driving one to do things that may not depict who one is. I usually tell my colleagues that it is a western culture feeling to think that the less you talk, the less intelligent you are. As discussed much deeper below, it is a folkloric feeling because in this culture, intelligence is usually associated with people who talk the loudest, seen all the time, people who are known, sound arrogant but in reality may not be (but other cultures may see them as such), and people who may be seem disrespectful, may be denoted to be so intelligent and frank. Instead of calling them out, they are rather described as people who *"call it as it is."* They describe them to be straight shooters and people who don't take nonsense.

Well, this is up for debate because in-between that assertion lies a certain true attitude of arrogance. There is nothing wrong with being a straight shooter; however, the manner in which you *"shoot"* is very important. I know of highly respected people in high places, who fall within this same culture who are straight shooters but not arrogant.

There is a young lady I know who is just phenomenal, unassuming but serves on various boards, knows people in very high places, and is known by them. Interestingly, she is an advocate and comes from a good home. I don't think money is an issue with her in the sense that her parents are well-to-do, and she herself is doing well. When you meet her the first time, you might disqualify her because of the way she speaks. She speaks calmly, slowly, and her voice comes across sometimes younger than she looks, but guess what, she is full of wisdom and courage and is very fascinating. She too is a westerner and from the same culture, but she is different. She is not like everyone else; she is unique. This is the reason we don't put everyone in the same basket.

I once told a friend that he would need to learn a lot more to be able to work in another country other than the western world because the lifestyles in most parts of the world and in different cultures are the total opposite of what we experience here. This is what you experience when you become or are made a global leader, overseeing people in different cultures, countries, and continents. If you have one approach for all, there will be chaos.

I remember working in a global company with most of our colleagues all over the world. While some of us in one part of the region work all week, Monday to Friday, with a maximum three weeks yearly vacation, others in the same company but in other regions work mostly four days a week, Monday to Thursday, usually took Friday off, and enjoyed more than six to eight weeks of vacation. Ironically, most people in those regions often perform better than those of us who work more days. The lesson to learn here, is that once you leave the borders of your culture, country, or continent, you must put on a different hat in order to fit in.

I have learned many cool things in every culture. There is no doubt about this, but as the saying goes, all things are permissible, but not all things are good for you. I chose the best. I chose what is good for me. I chose what would benefit me as I continue in my pursuit of life. By default, I love to smile most times because it makes me happy, but I also have my days when I am totally opposite of that. This is dependent on the day, mood, atmosphere, and the people around. Laughter and smiles are medicinal as far as I am concerned. I believe it's a natural no-wrinkles solution for your face, making you look younger while reducing stress, boosting your energy levels, reducing your blood pressure, and strengthening your immune system. This is just according to what I believe. Try it, friends—it works. What else do you want? Do you want to carry the world on top of your shoulders? Before you were born, the world already existed, full of its blessings, challenges, benefits, issues, and chaos. Why then make yourself the world's burden carrier? You can only do what you can within your lifetime and with whatever opportunity you may have.

During my teenage years, I was the exact opposite as far as smiling and creating a welcoming face was concerned. Someone who wouldn't laugh or smile, I was what people describe as "a stone-faced" person until I decided one day to wake up and become a better me. In the early 1990s, when I developed a personal relationship with God, I told my spirit to let go of the past. I was raised in a religious home and so had always known God, but I did not have that personal relationship with Him. These are two separate situations, but a lot of people do not know that one can be raised in a Christian home but still need to have a personal relationship with God to curve your path. My take is, it is better to be in chains for Christ than be free for the devil. My life changed and turned around for good. I choose smiling because you wouldn't want to see the other side. I hate to do things haphazardly, and I didn't want to be lukewarm, believing either you are hot or cold, so I preferred to persevere in showing my better self while I sank the ugly one gradually. I still get occasional visits from the past but never grant a chair for it to stay long.

This issue of trying to be like someone else happens also in the workplace, where women especially want to shoulder with the men to be identified and seen as hard-core. They want to prove that what men do, women can do, and even do better. I believe this was reemphasized during the famous 1996 Beijing conference to empower women. It was observed in the past (mostly) that some women sometimes wore clothing and hairstyles that disguised their bodies so as to portray themselves as "hard-core" personalities. This was all to achieve the goal of attaining high positions as men did, and I applaud that effort.

Today, we have numerous and very successful women leaders across the globe. I am not here to determine whether this is because of past efforts, but certainly there must be an iota of truth in any assertion that the hard work, dedication, and sacrifice of the pioneering and current advocates certainly helped. What you need is to be you. There are female combatants that sometimes perform better than their male counterparts. Just be you. There are some ladies that work harder than men, while such men sit in couches and watch television. This reminds me of the special strength women are granted to take care of children. I don't mean in any way that is their duty, but just the way they do it and how they do it is so special. While the men, including me, are already exhausted within minutes of spending time with the kids running around and with all the noise in the house, these women could do the same thing for weeks, months, and years with hardly a complaint. Just be you.

In His special wisdom, God places certain people in our way for special reasons, and it is our duty to determine what those reasons are. However, there are challenges and hurdles to climb. A friend once told me that from the day you're born, both your devil and your angel are born as well. It is your role to preserve the good side, allow good things into yourself, and then reap the fruit of your destiny, instead of the other way around.

LEARN AND KNOW YOURSELF

Sometimes you can experience two non-identical personalities from one person, and it is your duty to stand firm to the test and emerge victorious. Most times, we all have these types of multiple personalities: no wonder you see someone act in a totally negative manner one day, then on another day, that same person acts like an angel. This is minus people who act as hypocrites; they know exactly what they are doing. This is also different from people acting professionally in a separate setting, then fumbling in another setting. There is a fine line between these, and it is crucial to identify the differences.

In my observation, people who just act in ways that they themselves cannot comprehend or remember and then act completely different another time when in their conscious mind, they may be acting as have multiple-personality disorder (a terrible and painful disorder) in which they aren't. Be wary of such people, and if there is anything you can do to help them, please do. They need help.

I have been blessed to be surrounded mostly with people who just accept me for who I am. Interestingly, the same personality that attracts others like 'bees', puts others off. Be who you are but look for wisdom what people have to say and why. Do some self-reflection and decide if you needed and to what degree? All can be done without changing your personality, which is priceless. In life, you cannot please everyone, nor can you serve two masters. You would definitely obey one more than the other. I am a good dancer (metaphorically, though I can take some few steps), and I dance to the tune played by others. I am a naturally friendly person, I know how to create relationships and maintain them, I know how to make people laugh and sustain it, and I know how not to be boring and how to constantly stay dynamic. Nonetheless, I know also how to avoid people or a bad environment. I believe in applying wisdom on a daily basis on how to maintain friendship because you cannot use the same recipe for the same food all the time and expect a different result. People go through different emotional situations every second, and the same that might have been very interesting to them only yesterday might be a total nuisance the next day. Consider sharing a wonderful joke that threatened to break everyone's rib in laughter, only to find that the same joke angered people the next day. There could be factors accounting for this. Who knows? Some may have gone through the emotional stress of having a child that was ill, spouse not returning that call, mother not blessing that relationship, a bad dream, miscarriage, immigration issues, business contract not signed, indecision whether to go ahead with a decision or not, a breakup, swing of moods, and the list goes on and on and on. All of these could play a factor in creating someone's mood. Knowledge of these factors helps to enhance one's relationship with all. This lends assent to the position that wisdom should play a critical role in one's relationship.

America, that is regarded as the land of opportunities is also a place where you could experience the good, the bad, and the ugly, depending on which path you desire to carve for yourself. It is a place you either make it or do not. It is the land where a billionaire could be your next-door neighbor but may not be known as a billionaire, compared to other countries where everyone will have to know him or her. You can succeed if you put your head down. The choice is yours. This is where the cradle of business, education opportunities, and everything else including freedom resides, compared to other nations. This is where technology exists. This is where you meet people from diverse cultures that live in the same country. This is where most of the richest people on the planet live. This is where criminals exist as well. This is where the poorest also exist, and this is where there are more homeless people existing compared to other countries statistically, and where most natural disasters occur. You need to align yourself to the right side so to fall in great hands as destined for your life. There are some things you cannot avoid, but some are clearly orchestrated by humans and could be avoided. Learn the difference and stay right.

FOOD FOR THOUGHT:

Sometimes we forget that the expectations of someone else are not the same as another's. I have seen the good, the bad, and the ugly, but through the worst, I always came out victorious. Victory, to me, is determined by how you manage yourself, how you carry yourself in times of adversity, how you speak, and how you defend yourself. Make no mistakes, the best form of defense is to work smarter and harder rather than talking loudly. I was determined to never disappoint people who believed in me, let alone myself, my reputation, and the dignity that I had built up all the years. What is important is your gut feeling, especially when you have given it all. What you feel may not be what others may feel, so allow only your gut to speak to you, and if it says good job, run with it, because never will you enjoy full appreciation from a human being. If you are waiting to be told what you desire, you may sit there and rot because most people work for their own selfish gains. I know it takes a minute to damage twenty years of reputation that you have built, so having this in mind, it is good to be cautious. In times of difficulty, learn to coil into your shell, refocus, and find a way to deliver beyond your expectation. In the end, some of your critics may shower praises on you for the excellent job you've done. Remember also that in life, some people may be brought your way to toughen you up. You don't need to hate them; rather, ask yourself what role is that person playing in your life and what is it that you need to learn from this person. Then pray for them and move on. I am grateful for everyone who has made life difficult for me, without knowing, they have made me a better person, wiser, smarter, stronger and actually, wealthier.

CHAPTER 4

Fetal Formation Process and Its Implications

I was watching one of these television show where individuals showcase their unique talent. During this segment, a young artist comes on the stage with a large canvas and begins to draw a figure that confused the judges and the audience. To the human eye, the artist was creating something basic (that anyone with one semester of art could make); there was simply nothing special about the piece. As this artist was focused on the piece, the first judge had enough and hit the buzzer to disqualify her. The remaining three judges watched on as she continued. You could make out a face, an odd nose - what looked like an ascot or an awkward looking tie. The face - not very appealing. The audience, not convinced laughed a little - she continued on. Then the next two judges hit the buzzer. One judge remained, the confused audience looked on, within seconds the final buzzer went off - all judges had disqualified her work. A few seconds later the artist rotated her canvas, added the final finishing touch - a powder substance to reveal the contrast - to the amazement of both the judges and the audience was an accurate representation of one of the judges face that she drew with perfection.

She had taken the audience through an amazing journey that they did not understand. It was only when she flipped the canvas to reveal her final art, that they realized that they just witnessed the creation of a masterpiece in the making. The entire room stood to their feet to give her a standing ovation for her amazing creation. One of the judges that disqualified her went to her on the stage to personally kiss her - a gesture to say I am sorry and I want the world to know that I have made a serious lapse in judgment.

Similar, the process of creating human life is a very sacred and special process, which is the same for all individuals. We are conceived and shaped for nine months and then birthed. Regardless if you descend from a rich or poor family, born in a manger or the queen's palace, with a silver spoon or a wooden fork, we all have one commonality; we go through the process of birth

Yes, studies indicate the type of nutrition the mother takes, contributes to the child's development. While that is true, the actual process stays unchanged. We all go through the stages of conception, development, and birth!

The process starts when the male sperm combines with the female egg - the moment of conception. At this stage, it is unclear what the tiny creation will look like, act like, think like. To the human eye, it's just a spec, just like an artist work described above.

At six weeks, research reveals that the fetus is no bigger than a lentil. By the seventh week, it is said that the baby is approximately the size of a pea, slightly bigger than the lentil but still very tiny. About eight weeks, however, the baby is said to be the size of a lima bean. I wish you could get a lima bean and see how it looks in terms of size and weight, and then compare it to this formation. Imagine seeing sports giants who also were once like this. Very incredible and fascinating. When it gets to the ninth week, the baby now looks like the size of a standard pinky toe. This is someone who could grow to carry you but is now very helpless now as a pinky toe. At week ten, it's a graduation stage from embryo to fetus. Now it is about the size of your index finger from its tip to the first joint. Jumping to week twelve, whatever it is in there, will now start looking and forming like a human being. Just like a sketch, you can now start identifying its features. At week thirteen, the baby can now fit into your palm, but still, imagine how tiny that is. Jumping to week twenty-three, you need to be more careful what you say around the fetus because they can hear you. They identify voices and start movement. This is where when daddy returns from 'wherever' and the baby hears his voice, it starts slight movement in the tummy. On a lighter note; Daddy's, be good and nice to

FETAL FORMATION PROCESS AND ITS IMPLICATIONS

your ladies, else the baby knows and might coil on you. This is fascinating; however, a lot of people miss out on this vital process due to ignorance or personal challenges. The process and the journey, as far as I am concerned, are equally important like the destination or the result. This is the best stage in the child's development: you say positive things, sing, recite poems, pray with the baby, let mom watch beautiful programs, and read nice things around. You may experience its movement in the womb while you do this sometimes. This is the actual beginning of a child's education even before they come out. At week twenty-four, the baby is said to be about the size of a foot long. I hope you are with me here! This process continues throughout the weeks until that beautiful day when that child pops out. It is easier said that way, but the mother had to go through great pain and an entire delivery process to get that baby out. When that delivery day comes, this is when irresponsible men are insulted, and mothers vow not to give birth again; however, a few months later, the same process begins again.

Writing this reminds me of the first time I was asked to cut an umbilical cord. It was my first son's. I was scared to death. I never liked and still do not like contact with blood, let alone cutting something so tender and fleshy. But for the sake of my son, I went through with it.

When a baby is born, the genetics from the parents are mixed up in that baby, where related activities gained from the parents and lineage start to build up. This is where the giants are separated from the dwarfs in terms of the stature of that baby, brain growth and attitude are derived as they grow, all depending on the environment that child is brought under.

FOOD FOR THOUGHT:

This process shows us how humble we all should be in life. Regardless of the color of your skin, where you are born (for which you didn't contribute or have the opportunity to decide), how you were born, or to whom you were born, we are all almost the same in the way we were born. For those who did not have the perfect formation as it should be, it is the onus of all of us to come together to love, cherish, protect, and care for them and be their guardians. It hurts me to see such people humiliated and treated as second-class citizens. I have deep passion for a certain class of people—the destitute, people with disabilities, the aged, and especially children who suffer such ailments. We are perfectly imperfect and that's ok. It will take collective effort to make this world a better place to live and have a place to enjoy it.

CHAPTER 5

Time for Everything

One of my favorites passages in the Bible is in Ecclesiastes. This passage talks about seasons in life. The old saying *"there is a time for everything under the sun"* originates here. My understanding is that you can do the right thing at the wrong time and vice versa. How do you, therefore, know what time to do what? Ecclesiastes 3:1–8 in the New International Version, states:

"a time to be born and a time to die, a time to plant and a time to uproot, a time to kill and a time to heal, a time to tear down and a time to build, a time to weep and a time to laugh, a time to mourn and a time to dance, a time to scatter stones and a time to gather them, a time to embrace and a time to refrain, a time to search and a time to give up, a time to keep and a time to throw away, a time to tear and a time to mend, a time to be silent and a time to speak, a time to love and a time to hate, a time for war and a time for peace".

Wow, what a statement! This is not necessarily to be taken entirely in its literal form but is very true to the core.

What this verse is simply saying is that the right atmosphere will determine what to do. In order to gear you up, analyze the following scenarios and determine what to do in every situation.

Scenario 1: Imagine waking up in the morning preparing to go to work, only to receive an urgent call from your doctor that, based on your last visit, you are diagnosed with cancer. How would you handle the day at work?

Scenario 2: Imagine being told by your cousin earlier that your best friend had miscarried, upon inquiry and while you immediately rushed to be with your best friend to affirm it, only to receive a call later back from the doctor's office saying that it was a mistake and that the earlier test was not done properly. The doctor's office revealed your best friend was rather three months pregnant? How would your day go?

Scenario 3: Consider embarking on a project at work and receiving praises throughout the entire project until the end only to be betrayed by the same people who praised you. How would you feel or react?

Your reaction to any of the above scenarios may differ from person to person. Divorce, loss of job, death, abuse, and overly analyzing circumstances contribute to one's attitude in a given day. It is therefore good not to quickly judge someone or define someone's behavior by one's action. Or best put, don't judge them by a specific incident - they may be having an off day or week.

Certain conditions drive someone's behavior differently, which goes to confirm that the same smile that triggered someone's joy yesterday may become toxic another day. Why? Because it may not be coming at the right time.

Timing is everything. Learn to adapt to situations and place yourself in the 'shoes' of others before jumping too early conclusions.

Consider this; when racism is pointed at a particular race in society, the denounced racism, insisting that all men are equal, but comes back home and practices tribalism. It's like the tortoise telling you, there's no need to run but lend him horses' legs and see. The horse may wait to be ridden but tortoise would not wait even to be ridden. With no one riding it, the same tortoise would flee. The poor claim the rich are vain but let a little money come the way of the same and you would see the true display of vanity.

The point is not to judge anyone until you wear that person's 'shoes'. Your time will come to understand.

The actions and inactions of people are not necessarily based on their principles but more on their situation. People engage in acts that they do not necessarily believe in personally but feel they must do for their situation. As well, the situations in which people make their decisions may be different.

This is one reason you should not just jump to conclusions about anybody until you navigate the entire 360-degree angle of what may have driven the thought process.

Learn to tell the difference between the circumstantial errant and the diabolical liar, the double-faced hypocrite, the deliberately malicious, and purposeful assailant.

"A visionary born in the wrong time may seem like a pompous buffoon" (*"What Makes a Leader,"* Harvard Business Review). Just like someone living ahead of his time. Nichola Tesla might be a good example. Though not seen as a buffoon, he did come across as crazy. He believed you could transmit electricity long distances wirelessly. This was unheard of in a time where there was barely advancement in electricity. His work has lead to many of the technological advancements in electricity. Alternating Current vs Direct Current, The Adams Power Plant Transformer House- Buffalo NY., The induction motor. He has many other crazy ideas that are now being researched like transmitting electricity wirelessly and safely over long distances. This lead to the inspiration for wireless charging units - only a matter of time before they crack the code (if they haven't secretly cracked it already). Not to mention that Tesla car company is named after him. Who would think that in the next twenty years, we would have so many electric cars on the road - Elon was not afraid to look crazy.

It is important to know when to be quiet and when to talk as indicated above. Unfortunately, most people fall short by doing the right thing at the wrong time. Imagine falling in love with a pretty young lady and weighing the decision to take her out and when. Instead of waiting for the perfect time when the mood is right, just because you have it on your calendar (not hers), even when her mother is sick at the hospital and she needs attention and sympathy, you still go ahead and ask her out.

I don't need to be prescient to tell you that you will miss out on such an opportunity. She might even hate you and describe you as insensitive and probably not someone she would risk being in a relationship with, in the first place. Waiting a bit, taking her with you to see her sick mother, buying some flowers, and being present when she needed it would have done the magic.

Imagine seeking a job and craving every day about it but never taking one second to review the poor grammar in your application. When it is time to go for the interview, instead of preparing and researching the interviewing company and seeking experts' advice and guidance on what to do and what not to do, you would rather spend the time on unfruitful ventures but expect a miracle.

Imagine crossing a busy road without watching, and because of your faith, you believe no vehicle could knock you down. Trust me, you would be hit much harder than an unbeliever because you need to use your brains. The best and wisest option is to watch and run as fast as you can and be safe.

There is this story of a young girl who returned from school very hungry, and to her surprise, she found food on the table and started eating it. Deciding to steal it wholly, she concealed it. When she was queried about it, she denied ever setting eyes on the food. It was all because she hadn't asked in the first place.

The irony is, the food was actually hers, so invariably, she was stealing her own lunch unknowingly. When she realized it all, she broke down and confessed because it made her feel very bitter about herself.

All she should have done was to ask.

FOOD FOR THOUGHT:

Do what is right at the right time and know the difference. You don't wear a tux to a beach party, nor do you wear swimming suit to a black-tie event. It is crucial to know the timing for what to do and what not to do. A lot of people get frustrated for being paid back evil for doing good, but they probably took action too early or too late.

USING TIME EFFECTIVELY AND EFFICIENTLY:

When I started work post Master's degree so many years ago, I realized I had no spare time to do anything. I was juggling a new job, family and everything you can imagine at the time. I didn't have time to read anything apart from that of work-related stuff, I couldn't socialize, and I couldn't mingle the way I wanted to. After a few weeks, I devised a strategy because I knew if I continued on that path, I might retire with grey hair, as I worked hard but needed to be smarter. What I started to do was manage my time well. I sometimes had lunch in my car while I read a book at work. I watched television programs and connected with other colleagues while exercising at the work gym during midday before getting back to my desk. I made it a practice to make time and find it where necessary to make myself happy, and it worked very well.

Starting a new job is challenging in itself. Not only do you have to prove your work to others, you also need to build confidence, and develop a work cadence to make yourself more efficient - this all takes time. Rather than working hard, you need to work smart and find the most efficient way to do the work, build confidence, and build solid relationships.

I had to work on personal things overnight, during holidays, and on weekends. It paid off because my wife and I were able to spend time together, plan future ideas, and enjoy every bit of it. It was the time when websites were a big deal, it was in its early adoption stages so we were able to work on a number of them personally to build a private business. My wife worked mostly on it, and I would jump on it when I got home and work further on it for a long time into the night. I kept counseling myself that *"if you really want to make it through life, do not rely on just your paycheck, get some side life-changing investment in place."*

On the job, however, I made sure I got to work early and was usually among the last to leave. I believe in not being the first to always set out of the doors since that could impede your promotion even if you worked hard or smart—at least, not at the early stage of employment where perception is so crucial. I believed in my capabilities and in myself and was learning fast. I created a project plan timeline on every deliverable, be it for work or personal achievements and because I had a timeline with them, I was able to accomplish most of the deliverables and milestones. Not many people will like you, for whatever reason they may have, my policy is, disagree with me but do not disrespect me. With this principle in mind, I was able to overstep any hurdle that was in front of me, some of which strengthened and catapulted me to higher degrees. I am truly grateful for those who made life difficult for me along my career path because without knowing it, they made me stronger.

You may be hard-pressed on every side, but you may not be crushed yet, perplexed but not despaired yet, persecuted but not abandoned yet, struck down but not destroyed yet, so why spend time worrying? I went through fire, but little did they know they were baking me to taste better. Usually in a battle, the moment you get to the fiercest point, it signifies more closeness to the end than you think. This happens for instance when you are watching a movie, whenever you reach the point where the battle is tougher, stronger, nicer, then remember the end is near, it may not be long until the start of the victory song. Through all the battles and obstructions on my way, I refused to allow them to obstruct me. Indeed, sometimes the bullets might make you stagger for a while, but do not give up, keep moving, keep your focus, and do not allow any bad experience to destroy your total vision. Focus, focus, and focus on only the goalpost, do not veer from what is ahead of you, watch only the prize, and keep running.

FOOD FOR THOUGHT:

Be grateful for everyone along your path. Though some may not mean it well for you, be wise to learn whatever you need to learn from that person and move on. Also, managing time comes with prioritization of your activities, schedules, and executing schedules on time. Avoid procrastination by performing what needs to be done at a particular time. Life comes with its everyday schedules, and each day is new, so be prepared for it. In the midst of all this, create time to have fun along the way. That too calls for planning. Not everyone is born to plan or is organized; however, the least you can do is plan ahead of time. Learn to use your calendar, especially on your cell phone. Let it remind you a day, a week, a month, a few hours ahead of your planned activity. It works.

CHAPTER 6

Be the Best at What You Do— Success Has No Particular Path (Part 1)

Success is not only defined by the amount of wealth you possess, but also by the impact one makes in the lives of other people and society at large.

Consider Bill Gates, Michael Dell, Oprah Winfrey, Barack Obama, Nelson Mandela, Maya Angelou, and Roger Federer as just a few examples. All of these people took different paths towards their success. Some through education, some politics, some through investment, some with no education, others through journalism, some inherited their wealth and success from their parents, and some through sports.

They all have created a huge impact and conquered in their area of expertise. Let's have a quick 'drive' through the lives of some of these people and others below:

William Henry (Bill) Gates, may be known as one of the richest persons in the world, but he had to overcome a few challenges and bad habits to become who he is. In his own words during a speech to the students at the University of Nebraska-Lincoln's College of Business Administration, he admitted been a heavy procrastinator. This habit continued even when he was an undergraduate student at Harvard University. He missed classes, procrastinated till the very last minute before studying for exams. Eventually, he became a college dropout. A few years later, specifically on December 13, 1977, Gates was arrested in Albuquerque New Mexico for driving without a license and ran a red light. Despite all of the above, he rose to become a business magnate.

Gates became one of the youngest billionaires with his own wealth at the age of twenty-one, is seen and will always be remembered as a business tycoon, philanthropist, founder of Microsoft and one of the richest person's in the world. Bill and his wife Melinda have devoted to spending the rest of their life traveling the globe doing charity in deprived communities. They are impacting the lives of many through their charitable foundation. They are into education, grants, eradicating AIDS from the planet, and spending millions of dollars in Africa, India, and some deprived areas for this purpose. This is his new passion, and this is what he pursues for happiness. This is what satisfies him. He is not just rich from a distance; people actually enjoy some of his riches through many foundations that he has set up. He has so far spent from his own pocket more than forty billion US dollars ($40B USD) as revealed when he appeared for the first time on Ellen DeGeneres' show in February 2018, along with his twenty-one-year-old daughter.

No wonder Warren Buffet connected with the Bill and Melinda Gates Foundation by donating to continue the good work. Warren's philosophy is, if he cannot do what the Gates do, his wealth can do it through them. This is simply the essence of commonality.

"By acknowledging and accepting the ultimate commonality, we can naturally and voluntarily develop the attitude of compassion and benevolence toward other people, other life-forms, and all beings. We will want to live for the good of all because we know that's the way we benefit ourselves, too."

- Ilchi Lee, Change: Realizing Your Greatest Potential.

Oprah Gail Winfrey is described as the richest African American of the twentieth century and one of the most philanthropic of all time, but she was sadly a rape victim when she was very young. She was sexually assaulted at a young age of nine (9) by a nineteen (19) years cousin, and later a family friend and an uncle. She spent most of her tender years with her grandmother until when she became ill that they had to move Oprah to her mother. Her mother worked menial jobs as a maid and had to rely of welfare to support them. Oprah had to move from one place to another for a number of years due to hardship and circumstance. In spite of these and many others, she defiled the odds in her life to rise above the stars.

As a media mogul and one of the most influential females of all time, she also was once the world's only black billionaire, and arguably, is one of the most successful women in the world as of now. Winfrey personally donates more of her own money to charity than any other celebrity in America. In 2005 she became the first black person listed by Business Week as one of America's top fifty most generous philanthropists. This has inspired her large network to contribute to her cause. In the wake of Hurricane Katrina, Oprah asked her viewers to open their hearts, and they did. As of September 2006, donations to the Oprah Angel Network Katrina registry totaled more than eleven million US dollars ($11 million). Homes have been built in four states—Texas, Mississippi, Louisiana, and Alabama—before the one-year anniversary of Hurricanes Katrina and Rita. Winfrey also matched her viewers' donations by personally giving ten million US dollars ($10 million) to the cause.

Winfrey has also helped two hundred and fifty African American men continue or complete their education at Morehouse College in Atlanta, Georgia.

In 2004, Oprah and her team filmed an episode of her show entitled Oprah's Christmas Kindness, in which she and her partner Stedman Graham as well as her best friend Gayle King, and some crew members traveled to South Africa to bring attention to the plight of young children affected by poverty and AIDS epidemic.

Most recently, she appeared on CNN's Van Jones show where she revealed that she does a lot good stuff to people behind the scenes and does not want it to be publicized. She also sometimes personally calls people in need and helps them quietly, asking them to not mention her name (as revealed on the Van Jones Show in 2018).

When asked by Mr. Jones what about her family and relatives, Oprah in her usual smiling and jovial manner stated, there is no problem about that, and that she takes extremely good care of them all, because they don't have any issues whatsoever.

The point here is not what you already know, but rather the generosity behind what she does. It is easier for Oprah to raise money than you and me because companies, individuals and other philanthropists trust and to have something in common with her. Thank goodness she uses it well.

Nelson Madiba Mandela, was a political magician who can be described by '3 p's': prisoner, president, and peacemaker. A notable man who laid down his life for the freedom of his country, Mandela spent almost three-fourths of his life in prison but rose to become the first elected president of South Africa between 1994 and 1999.

Mandela was one of the few unique leaders who promised a one- term leadership regime and he kept to it. He was also wise by convincing his opposers to work with him for the sake of peace and good for the nation they all claimed to love together.

Many refer to Mandela as a model to reckon with. Mandela was known to be a wealthy person in spirit, and through his achievements, to an appreciable extent, he bridged the racial divide. The legendary musical composer Philip Handel said that black and white must work together to form a good sound. He was then referring to the colors of the piano, indicating that without both colors, it would not produce a great sound. Mandela did just that. Mandela's name and quotes are on many school and office buildings and homes, and it is carried with pride and with full respect. His impact on the planet is still fresh and so significant that many politicians emulate him. In his own words, *"during my lifetime, I have dedicated myself to the struggle of the African people. I have fought against white domination, and I have fought against black domination. I have cherished the ideal of a democratic and free society in which all persons live together in harmony and with equal opportunities. It is an ideal, which I hope to live for and to achieve. But if need be, it is an ideal for which I am prepared to die."*

What seems impossible can be reversed, so stop excuses and do something about your life. Whilst in prison, Mandela undertook study with the University of London. By correspondence through its external study program, he received a Bachelor of Laws. He was subsequently nominated for the position of Chancellor of the University of London in the 1981 election, but lost to Princess Anne. Even in jail, he maintained focus on his purpose. While some leaders earned their reputation by intimidating and hurting other inmates in jail, Mandela grew his reputation by being genuine, increasing his knowledge, staying dedicated to his vision and treating others with respect. These were the pillars that lead him to become widely known as the most significant black leader in South Africa.

In February 1985, President P.W. Botha offered Mandela conditional release in return for renouncing armed struggle. Coetzee and other ministers had advised Botha against this, saying that Mandela would never commit his organization to give up the armed struggle in exchange for personal freedom. Mandela indeed spurned the offer, releasing a statement via his daughter Zindzi saying, "What freedom am I being offered while the organization of the people remains banned? Only free men can negotiate. A prisoner cannot enter into contracts."

All of his sacrifices and achievements combined means nothing if he did not translate them into touching the lives of many underprivileged people in society across the globe. A lot of people from diverse races try to emulate his lifestyle to do something in society. In his owner, his words and quotes are cited everywhere.

Roger Federer, known as the best tennis player of all time in this era, is simply a sports gentleman. From racquet-smashing enfant terrible with a bad attitude and ill-advised ponytail to a universally respected sporting role model and modern icon, Roger Federer has come a long, long way - news@thelocal.ch, Dave James/AFP.

Who, ever remembers and knows the latter part of his life? Not many, because he had to work at it to bury the old - impatient behaviors to a totally new person he is now. Look at him now.

He is one of the few players that divide the loyalty of the audience even when he plays a host nation's best player. Many, love him, not just because of the wins but also for the way he carries himself. Attitude, humility, composure, gentleness, and friendliness combine to make him very admirable. Having held the number one spot for a quite a few years in the past, many sports analysts, tennis critics, and former and current players consider Federer to be the greatest tennis player of all time.

Roger has played with different people, with different styles, and in different eras. Styles in terms of how they curl the balls, to playing long hours, as a result increasing stamina, into speed of 'serving', Roger has seen it all.

SYNERGY AND COMMONALITY

He has his pitfalls as any human being, but Federer is regarded as one of the best sports personalities the world has ever had. It is exciting to know that he is no superhero but a human being who just decided to be special and different in his adult life. Federer's successes and admiration can be described in different facets that include, first and foremost, how he handles himself even under pressure down to the obvious, and his career successes.

As a sports person, he has taught many people how to remain calm under pressure even when things aren't going one's way. It is very fascinating that while fans watching him play may feel heartbroken because he is losing a match, the one who is actually losing the real prize money is so calm, relaxed, and plays every point as though he was in practice—and finally wins. To date, he still carries himself as a symbol to be reckoned with.

On a charity front, it has become his second nature.

Roger is also making huge impacts through dozens of charitable initiatives across the globe, including Africa, China, Europe, and the Americas just to mention a few.

Venus and Serena Williams, who also need no introduction, have defied the odds and played tennis as if they emerged from the womb with a tennis racket in hand. Their rise to the greatest heights in sports history is nothing short of fascinating!. Venus and Serena are two of a kind. What is the more admirable about them is how they support each other. The only time you see them competitive is when they are playing against each other.

Despite their success, they were brought up from a tough neighborhood where they saw and heard gunfire's all the time. They went through economic depression, hunger and had a very difficult life at an early age. Their father sensing trouble, decided to introduce them to playing tennis to occupy their minds. They started excelling pretty fast and so, this venture became their lifestyles which we see the fruits today.

Serena has become the queen of tennis. Oh wow, this lady has proven that no matter what you throw at her, she will play and play and play and focus to win. She is a winner by all standards.

I have seen Serena out seeded in the tennis ranks, however, she clawed and jumped back from injury to win all majors in one year. Her power, speed, skills, stamina and never give-up-spirit have taken her to all imaginable heights. People who are not fans of hers have found themselves sitting by, watching, as she triumphantly swept game after game with an unbeatable grin on her face. Through the reality of upsets, hardships, and injuries, Serena has persevered to find success. The name Serena Williams has an automatic association to "winner," and that is all that matters.

She and her sister have invested in many ventures, knowing that tennis may not be there to produce wealth for them forever. They are dedicated to giving back to society. I recall seeing both sisters visiting their native home Nigeria, playing a charitable game to support girls, and Venus winning that match gallantly. It's beautiful watching how they grew from children to adults, and how they grew to be amazing athletes strong as well in the game, and charitable. This, I call wisdom.

They both separately or together supported numerous organization (either individually or together) such as the American Heart Association, American Stroke Association, Elton John's AIDS Foundation, Save the Music Foundation, Great Ormond Street Hospital, the Heart Truth. The Serena William Fund (or "SWF") was created to address persistent problems such as gun violence, educational inequity, and poverty that have personally impacted her family.

Maya Angelou was a famous poet, author, actress, and philanthropist. Getting to know more about this great lady proves that when you research, read, and make a conscious effort to educate yourself, you often come across information which you may otherwise never have seen.

While researching Maya Angelou, I discovered the resounding poet had been a dancer, educator, fry cook, television producer, journalist, actress, and film director. This great person survived the crossroads of racism and sexism all through her life. Maya even had to work at some point in her life as a sex worker to survive and went through a lot of difficult times growing up. Who cares now?

However, Maya is best known and recognized worldwide as one of the greatest African American poets and authors in history.

Since I am privileged to have an elder brother Richard, who is a writer and a journalist, I have known this remarkable lady's work since I was a child, but research has added more 'meat' to my knowledge. I can state confidently, therefore, about her influence.

In 1969, Angelou published her memoir *"I Know Why the Caged Bird Sings"* that earned her the respect as a new kind of author in the autobiography genre. She redefined the experience for black women writers by showing them how to act as central characters in their own works, for the first time. But Angelou didn't just redefine this experience for black female writers. She also freed many other women by writing about her childhood experience, sexuality, and racism. Through this work, Angelou has become one of the most highly respected African American female writers in its era.

Maya until her death, had impacted many lives across the globe. Her portraits and words of wisdom in 'quotations' are hanging in many homes, offices, and buildings all over the world. Her poems are used in movies and speeches. Her legacy lives on, due to the power of her influence throughout her lifetime. This is what we should aspire to – living a life of significance rather than success. Making a mark in people's lives that will continue to exist in a timeless form. Maya has created unknown heroes and a sense of commonality amongst many poets who desire to be like her. What is important is to be you and create your own name but continue to learn from the experts to become a better you in your area of expertise.

Barack Obama, love him or hate him, has created a unique storyline regardless of your political affiliation. Barack Obama had many things going against him when he decided to run for president of America. He's a black man with Kenyan-Indonesian heritage, a suspicious name (given the political climate), with little political experience going up against a political powerhouse (the Clintons), against a legacy of white Caucasians dominated presidency. He fought against all those odds to win the presidency of the free world.

I have described Obama to many friends as someone who dared to climb a huge mountain and safely reached its heights.

I look at it first from his name—a name that sounds close to Osama—at the time when this tyrant was the most wanted terrorist on the planet. Obama was able to pull through this to win the presidency with his name. That was a remarkable achievement, which some people overlook. I truly respect the country for the opportunity given to him, as this goes to prove that, in America, everything is possible. However, I am not done with him yet. He was able to climb the initial stages by beating other Democratic competitors, including someone with the last name Clinton, which was a household name, to win the party's nomination initially and later win the general election. When he won the party's nomination, it was believed that he was capable and close to winning the general election, and he did.

Another major point we need to remind ourselves is that he was black. This was another strike against him, but he pulled through this one too. We all believed that one day a black man could become the president of the United States, but never did most people believe it was possible at the time that Obama made it.

The last strike was his origin. Obama, an African American raised by a white mother, spent almost all his life in the US, but he is more of African descent than the other way around. This is because his father was a Kenyan, so he had no issues with his roots, unlike the sad story of most other African Americans whose great-great-great-grandparents were taken into slavery, and as a result, lost lineage and heritage to their true source. Obama, on the other hand, could be called an African, period! He could fly straight into his father's house in Kenya without any sweat nor roots research. Yes, he was raised by a white mother and later white grandparents, so technically, his mindset in terms of his upbringing was more 'whit-ish' than 'black-ish', I agree, but in context, he is an African, especially when the continent believes more in patrilineal heritage than matrilineal. Although his father played almost zero role in his life, he has maintained his name, Obama.

When you put your mind to something and believe in it, there is no mountain that you cannot climb, no barrier you cannot cross, and no height you cannot reach regardless of color, height, origin, religion, race nor creed. His middle name Hussein, to put butter on the bread for you, was another huddle that he needed to jump over. Hussein is a typical Muslim name, and as history revealed, there has never been a Muslim or anyone bearing a Muslim name considered to run for the seat of the United States presidency. Though he maintained that he was not a Muslim himself, rather a Christian, the fact that he has a name portraying a religion that says different makes it even more difficult for him to explain. He climbed that ladder and surged through this too. The point is, Obama evoked the dying spirits in many souls who have given up in whatever they were doing, just by the type of standards he has set through his unique and gifted speeches. In fact, with the strikes he had on him—a black man, the last name Obama, an African, the middle name Hussein, less experience in the

Senate, too young—everything was pointing negatively at him to lose the election, but he believed in himself and his potential. Though the black community and Latinos voted massively for him in terms of percentile basis, it was the whites, especially white women that actually put him into office because they form the mass majority statistically. This is a country of freedom and the land of opportunities indeed.

The impact and the hope he created in the lives of many young and the old generation across the world is undeniably phenomenal. Yes, he had his down times, and many, just like any other politician, may not accept some of his policies but he remains someone who has made a mark one way or the other. His name is all over the planet due to the history he's made. His name has become the household name in every part of this world, and when he speaks, people listen, whether you like him or not.

Amongst his speeches, he speaks a lot about a sense of unity, seeing each other as one, creating the spirit of commonality in the belief that all men are created equal. Even if you don't believe in all his principles, you will at least be motivated to listen to him. He is a captivating figure and will continue to be. This is the kind of impact he has created.

Note: part 2 of this discussion is on chapter 7 next.

CHAPTER 7

Be the Best at What You Do—Success Has No Particular Path (Part 2)

This chapter is a continuation from the previous chapter 6, with focus on some selected individuals who have made a difference by the way they live and conduct their lives as far as work ethic, and its associated success applies.

Michael Dell, is the founder of Dell Technologies. He may be the brainchild of a multi-billionaire dollar empire, but it didn't come cheap. He is the best to tell you how unglamorous it all started in a dorm as a nineteen (19) year old teenager and begun the company with just one thousand US Dollars ($1,000). In his own words, he was making up to eighty thousand US Dollars ($80,000) a month from that dorm. The rest is history. I think this should be a good lesson for young people starting a business. You don't need so much to start, you need focus, determination and the right partner(s) to surge.

Dell was not known for his academic excellence, but rather known for his computer business model 'germ'. He never stocked products or made computers ready to be sold (at the time). Rather, when you called to order a computer, the sales executive would interview you to determine your need. Your computer would then be created and customized for you in terms of specification and price. They would then take your credit card and take your money for the specification you agreed on. It was genius and a huge success. He literally was taking your money prior to creating your computer for you, thereby eliminating warehousing, storage fees, transportation issues, and inventory deficits. In business investment, we call that OPM strategy, meaning "Other People's Money". Dell was a college dropout, but he now hires the Ivy League scholars to work for him.

As a successful businessman, investor, philanthropist, and author, he received an Honorary Doctorate in Economic Science from the University of Limerick in 2002. This was in honor of his investment in the Republic of Ireland, the local community and support for educational initiatives.

With the passion to bring excellence in children's health and education in Austin - Texas, he granted a fifty million US dollars (£50 million) from the "Michael and Susan Dell Foundation" to support three key projects. These projects include; the Dell Pediatric Research Institute to compliment the new Dell Children's Medical Centre. The Dell Computer Science Hall, which was built on the University of Texas campus. The Michael and Susan Dell Centre for Advancement of Healthy Living, intended to support healthy childhood development.

In the early through mid-2000s, when you had a Dell computer, you belonged. You were automatically regarded as a genius or someone at the upper echelon of computer knowledge. Possibly, a lot of deals may be derived during that period by just a common factor, be in possession of 'Dell computers'. All you had to do was to own a Dell computer.

Again, my desire in this book is not to focus on his wealth but more on what he has done to impact society as stated above. It is to be noted, therefore, that these are just excerpts from what these and many giants have done and continue to do in society.

Tiger Woods: In spite of his personal challenges, for which we all have, one cannot dispute that he is one of the best golfers the world has ever produced. He remains one of the biggest sports icons. People looked up to him as he held the number one spot in golf for many years. He was also one of the youngest professional golfers the world has produced. Tiger came to the scene in 1996 while he was just about twenty-one years of age. He won both the PGA player and PGA tour of the year most part in 1997, 2003, 2005-2007, 2009 and 2013 respectively. He has won a lot of such conservatively like the PGA Tour leading money, Vendor trophies, and Byron Nelson awards, as well as many which cannot be highlighted in this book.

Tiger suffered from some personal challenges along his career and dropped in ranking to almost the very lowest but he remains genius, smart, and captivating. Tiger in a surprising career upset, won the 2018 tour championship. He may be on the verge of a big comeback as he is leading the headlines at the moment.

The resiliency, persistence, the 'never-give-up' personality and his hunger for success are what is helping him. The best part, he gives back a lot in charities.

LeBron James is a name that has come to stay. There have been many basketball players in recent times that truly made names, like the undisputable Kobe Bryant, Shaq, and most recently, the unstoppable Stephen Curry, who have stepped up to join such a unique club. However, LeBron James is arguably an exception in his own right. Having studied his background, how he rose to the top is phenomenal. A lot of people may not know that he started playing at a very young age on a team in Ohio called the Irish. It was a team of five best players who came together and won many tournaments, even against the most respected teams at the time and made their name in the process. One of the only times they lost a major tournament as a young group was when they became overconfident and too sure of winning. Of course, they were used to winning, so they wouldn't listen to their coach. As a result, they lost. When they regrouped, accepted their defeat and the reason for it, they did what was necessary, played as a team, and regained their title before their time was due for college. While some of his teammates had scholarships to play football or basketball and others had international opportunities in basketball, LeBron declined to go to college. He instead joined the Cleveland Cavaliers.

After playing in Cleveland for about eight years without an NBA title (a championship ring), he decided to move to a different team. It was one of the most dramatic seasons the basketball world had ever experienced—the anticipation, the anger from his teammates, and boiling rage from fans. Before declaring his decision to join the Miami Heat in that memorable interview, he stated that he just wanted to win a title. He went on to win two titles within four years or so at Miami.

It became a fascinating story when he decided to go back home to Cleveland after the drama of his exit a few years ago. That too made huge news because hardly did such a transition occur in sports history for years.

When he went back, he promised the entire state that he had come to help the team win the championship title because, at the time, they hadn't won the title for about fifty years. He was able to take them on his wings the very first year to the Eastern Conference Finals, and the following three years after that. Finally, in 2016, they won their first national title. The Cleveland Cavaliers were down 3:1 to the Golden State Warriors, and they were playing the fifth game at the home of the Warriors. It was obvious the Warriors would win until the Cavaliers shocked them by winning the remaining three games in a heroic and unprecedented manner to take the cup in the Warriors home, just like the Warriors had done to them the previous year at the Cavaliers' home.

Arguably, LeBron is currently described as one of the best players of all time. This is because of the longevity of his career, the consistency, the improvements, the fact that he shares the ball, dribbles well, dunks best, blocks well, shoots best, and is regarded one of the best finishers of all time. Love him or hate him, he is just admirable to watch.

Aside from his skills, LeBron is heavily into charitable programs in support of people in need. He never forgot his beginning and where he comes from. This is a young guy who has never met his father before, and who was raised by a single mother. At a young age, they moved from place to place, sometimes at a record of more than five moves in two years. As a young boy, it was devastating and frustrating, but he never complained nor questioned his mother as most other young boys at his age would, according to his own words in an interview. He was always prepared with a small packed bag just in case they had to move again. His mental toughness has indeed brought him far in all aspects of life, not just in sports.

He has built a school in Akron, Ohio, and heavily into charitable projects, thereby spending millions of his US dollars just to make someone's life better.

...And so what? How do any of the above-mentioned characters have any effect on me?

The above-mentioned people are just a selected few. One thing we should understand is that their influence comes from diverse fields of expertise. You do not need to be a scholar to influence people, neither do you need to be rich to make an impact. Influence starts from your little sphere of authority, be it your home, your neighborhood, your family, workplace, and so on. Set a good example since every great step begins with a tiny one. Before you can run, you will need to learn how to crawl, then how to stand, falling in between many times, and then gradually start learning how to walk, then you can run eventually. Whatever you do, you will need people with similar aspirations to help you along the way. In order not to regress in life, you will need to affiliate yourself with the right people, learn, and train to increase your speed to the pace unique to you.

There are millions of people out there who, one way or another, influence somebody's life. From the tiniest contribution to a person who has to farm in order to provide food in a village somewhere in Africa, to the one who lives in the biggest city in the western part of the world, though their names may not be recorded or known, they are all there doing what they can to be a blessing to someone. Never forget anyone who at some point sacrificed something for you. Though it may not be big and significant, it was remarkable enough to contribute as part of the bridge to your success. I wonder why Jesus said in one of his parables that it will be easier for a camel to enter the eye of a needle than for a rich person to go to Heaven. In fact, when I read it at first, I misunderstood it to mean being rich was bad and deemed all rich people evil. The word 'rich' was figuratively used to mean that anything you value more than God is an idol because that same thing could be a hindrance to your success, at least to my understanding. Hoarding and not learning to share is part of the issue.

In all that you do, be the best that you can be; that is your recipe for success. Learn not to repeat mistakes if you can.

Thomas Edison, inventor of the light bulb, failed hundreds of times before he succeeded. A journalist at the time asked him why he never quit, and what he learned from all these experiences. Thomas simply said that he had learned how not to make a bulb over hundreds of times. Today, because of his persistent attitude, you and I have the most basic and common asset called light. Dwell on the positive while you increase your potential, never settle for what you know, practice more, read good and challenging books, surround yourself with people smarter than you and don't let it intimidate you, put yourself to the test, and always do better than you did yesterday. Otherwise, soon, everyone will catch up with you, and your value will be diminished.

While we spent some time discussing selected celebrities who made it to the top, with most rising from nothing to something, one great example of such achievers is the unforgettable Kevin Skinner.

The chicken farmer **Kevin Skinner** may not be a familiar name. I know most people reading this may wonder who this person is. This young man appeared on the television show 'America's Got Talent' in 2009 and gradually climbed the ladder to win the competition. During that season, there were many talented people in his group, and nobody gave him a chance, just by the way he appeared. He didn't have the looks, he didn't come from a fancy place, there was so much doubt around him, so just like others who only come to mess up, he was mentally cut into the category to do whatever he wanted to do and give way for others to perform. Kevin, however, believed in himself. The crowd and the judges seemed to intimidate him at first, as he seemed shaky, but he never gave up on his vision. Indeed, when he got onto the stage the first time, Kevin was a laughing stock. Even the judges, looking at their facial expressions, must have thought this was someone who would only waste everybody's time, based on the way he looked, dressed, and spoke. He aggravated the situation. When asked about his profession, he said he chased chickens. What? The whole audience, as well as the judges, burst into laughter upon hearing this. However, when Kevin opened his mouth and started singing, not only did he stun the audience, but the judges were flabbergasted. He brought tears to the eyes of many because he sang from his heart and not his lips. This chicken chaser went through all the rounds and gradually won the hearts of many, and he emerged the final winner of the show that year.

I believe Kevin won the entire competition not because he had the best vocals on stage, or evoked the best presence, but because he looked sincere and believable, and performed as one whom the American public was compelled to accept deserved the prize most.

Many are such individuals out there who made history just like Mr. Skinner and who may not be known and acknowledged but who are changing lives in their communities somewhere. They deserve all the praise, the kudos, and the accolades. Nothing is impossible, and if you focus and fix your mind, you can achieve anything you wish to. If you are someone who thinks your world has come to a halt and so there is no path for you, this boost is for you. If you are someone who possesses little confidence, this is for you. If you are someone who is laughed at and feel inferior wherever you find yourself, this is definitely yours to take. If you are someone whom everyone, including your loved ones, tells that you have no talent, this is just for you to soak in. If you are someone who is despised and who does not have a place in anyone's heart, please remember, this encouragement is to wake you up. If you allow another's negative perception to dictate your future, it will not go well with you. Don't let them win; instead, win over them.

FOOD FOR THOUGHT:

If you desire to succeed, desire also what it takes to get you there. Many people want the victory but do not want the pain that comes with it. Watch the grueling training sessions with any of the successful people you know, especially in sports, and you will appreciate the amount of time, energy, dedication, and toil that goes into it. I watched Usain Bolt's training session and was flabbergasted. The rigorous push-ups, running with weight and ropes on his waist, pulling him back, exercising in the hot sun bare-chested, obeying his strict trainer to the final 'letter' word, carrying metals, engaging in all sorts of training, sweating vigorously and profusely just for an under-ten-second victory. This goes on for hours upon hours to get his body in shape and conditioned for his race.

It takes discipline and fortitude to achieve your dream, and you cannot do otherwise and expect a different result. Consider others who are non-sports personalities like Bill Gates. This guy is an avid reader, always educating himself and learning from others. He probably reads a book a week to keep his brain active. Why should someone like him who has it all still read educational books? Recall the synergy math, i.e., $1 + 1 = 5$, not 2? This is what people like Bill Gates have accumulated in terms of compound effect in knowledge, and now his $1+1$ is now equal to a billion.

When you visit an icon, look around and see what he is reading, or what he or she is doing differently that is setting them apart. There is a reason why they control the world with their influence, wealth, and presence. It did not manifest overnight; it takes hard work, sleepless nights, and a typical brand of mindset. While over ninety percent of the world is sleeping, disciplined minds stay awake and go the extra mile to make a mark. Try it in whatever field you desire and see the type of result you will amass. It may not come as quickly or as easily as you want, but it will come with persistence.

CHAPTER 8

From Riches to Rags

While many celebrities strive during their careers to invest, thereby digging their wells before they get thirsty, some others have messed up their entire opportunities.

Let's take time to look at these selected few who could have made the most of their lives but blew it. In other words, who did not live out their full potential.

Former heavyweight champion, **Mike Gerard Tyson**, had it all at the beginning of his career, but then he lost all. A saying goes that it is much more difficult to climb than to fall. That was what happened to the former undisputed heavyweight icon. He had the fame, the punch, the physique, the money, and the success at a young age; however, due to mismanagement of his own life, he lost them all. I was a die-hard supporter of Mike and enjoyed seeing him fight, and I would do anything to go any length just to watch this brilliant guy fight at the time. I rooted for him. I even wept when he lost his fight against Buster Douglas in the eighth round. Tyson was my man and everybody's bet. Unfortunately, Mike's career started a downward spiral with an accusation of rape that affected his reputation, and his money started flying away. He had to file for bankruptcy in 2003. Can you imagine someone who was paid millions of dollars for a few seconds' long fight, now filing for bankruptcy? He never regained his career after all the damages. He tried a television program where he was featuring birds, but I don't know how those series ended. Probably it didn't attract the attention it needed to keep it going.

How could someone who had earned over three hundred million US dollars ($300 million) during his career as a boxer allow the excessive desire for jewelry, mansions, cars, limousines, cell phones, parties, clothing, motorcycles, and even owning Siberian tigers eventually catch up to him to ruin him? The bankruptcy in 2003 was inevitable, thanks to a colorful variety of debts including thirteen million, four hundred thousand US dollars ($13.4 million) to the internal revenue service (IRS) and a nine million US dollars ($9 million) divorce settlement to his ex-wife, Monica Turner. From 1995 to 1997, it was recorded that he spent millions of US dollars in legal fees, two hundred and thirty thousand US dollars ($230,000) on pagers and cell phones, and four hundred and ten US dollars ($410,000) on a birthday party. In June 2002, he owed eight thousand and one hundred US dollars ($8,100) in care for his tigers and sixty-five thousand US dollars ($65,000) for limos.

Mike Tyson's loss of fortune still remains unbelievable. No matter what has happened, however, he remains the "Iron" Mike Tyson.

Kim Basinger, one of Hollywood's highest earners in the late 1980s bought the entire tourist town of Braselton in Georgia for twenty million US dollars ($20 million). This tourist attraction venture did not yield any good result for Kim.

In a separate event in 1993, Kim made another wrong move by signing up to star in a movie, a decision she backed out from just four weeks to the film shooting. That resulted in Kim being sued. The controversial movie – "Boxing Helena" was about a surgeon who kidnaps and amputates the woman he is obsessed with. Kim was sued heavily for backing at a short notice.

In the end, she was forced to sell Braselton for only one million US dollars ($1 million) and forced to declare herself bankruptcy to settle the eight million US dollars ($8 million) supposedly in claims and debts.

Marvin Gaye, was raised in a decent home and grew to become one of the most remembered musical icons. He was successful both in fame and financially but due to bad decisions, he suffered a great loss.

He lost almost everything he had worked for, and so, was besieged by tax problems and drug addiction. Later on, the "Let's Get It On" singer filed for bankruptcy in 1979 and moved to Hawaii, where he lived in a bread van and began working on his album 'In Our Lifetime'. He was eventually shot by his priest father for what his father described as betrayal of the faith he brought him under.

It was a pity how his life ended, though his music is still alive in the minds of many.

Burt Reynolds declared bankruptcy in 1996 with six million, six hundred thousand US dollars ($6.6 million) in assets and eleven million, two hundred thousand US dollars ($11.2 million) in debts. He used to own mansions, a helicopter, and a lavish Florida ranch. However, when investments in two restaurant chains in the late 1980s and 1990s went bad, followed by a fall-off in his box-office clout, Bandit's finances suddenly went bust. In the end, he had to sell his trademark moustache at an auction to help pay his bills. Reynolds got to keep his two million, five hundred thousand ($2.5 million) Florida estate, however, a shining example of how bankruptcy proceedings go too easy on the wealthy, not the average.

Burt Reynolds did have a resurgence with Boogie Nights, and he seemed to be doing pretty well before his death. He is an exception but considering where he came from in terms of the type of wealth he had earlier, and how he lost them in a wind was devastating worth to mention, so to advice people of wealth management.

MC Hammer is another name worth mentioning. I grew up admiring this musician and a great dancer. I read magazines of him and his rise to fame, dance skills, and positive message in his music. We learned his dancing moves in school and everyone wanted to be like him at the time. However, having amassed debts of thirteen million US dollars ($13 million) due to bad investments and mismanagement of his wealth and filed for bankruptcy in 1996. Some of his past expenses included his modest California home— complete with two pools, a cinema, tennis courts, and seventeen-car garage. He also bought a helicopter, several racehorses, and a sound system that required twenty-two miles of wiring, not to mention the solid gold chains for his four pet Rottweiler's.

Hammer is said to be living today with his family to survive, at least at the time of my research. I have seen him on television ads recently though, but I don't know how that has catapulted him financially. He now juggles several careers as a rapper, television presenter, and preacher to support his family of six.

Gary Coleman, the once beloved, highest paid television child actor from Different Strokes filed bankruptcy in 1999 citing seventy-two thousand US dollars ($72,000) in personal debts. Things turned out so tough for Gary such that, in order to get himself out of his financial woes, he became the beneficiary of an internet charity that auctioned off items, such as his spatula, sofa, purple bowling ball, size four-and-a-half bowling shoes, and his self-described yellow pinstriped *"pimp suit."* He even held a contest in which the grand prize was a Christmas shopping spree—with Coleman serving as the winner's *"shopping elf."*

Times were tough for Coleman, and perhaps it was the financial stress that led him to punch a woman while working as a security guard at some point.

Watching **Vin Baker** on Steve Harvey show in recent time brought tears to my eyes notwithstanding the attendant joy. I felt sad about what he had going for him but which he couldn't put together and lost everything, and I also felt joy because he had found a better way forward. He was positive, had gotten back his wife and family, and was leading a decent life. Consider seeing this giant former NBA play - worth one hundred million US dollars ($100 million) in the 1990s, a former Boston Celtic star who appeared a consecutive four times at the All-Star Games, but whose career got damaged by substance abuse. He confessed to being an alcoholic, even drinking during practices. As I write this, he is working as a store manager for Starbucks. He has since changed and made amends with his wife and children and is becoming a great father. However, this was a one-time rich and rising star who just blew it. This is a big lesson no one should go through. In his interview with Steve Harvey, he said while serving a client coffee sometime, the client looked at him and immediately asked why he wasn't playing basketball with his height instead of using it serving coffee with it. He looked at her, just smiled, and left without uttering a word. Little did she know where he came from.

These are just a few examples of mismanagement of wealth and or personal life.

FOOD FOR THOUGHT:

A lot of people are interested in making money but are never prepared or coached on how to maintain that wealth. It is good to unlearn certain things in order to build a new sense of character. While a lot of people may admire and may desire to be like any of the characters above, little did they know what they were going through in life. This is why, although it's okay to desire to be like someone, aspire to be you, and then learn to be a better you by learning from people who have the right fruit on the tree. If you were to give any of the above individuals a second chance, they would have had a 180-degree life turnaround. Why not teach yourself to be proactive rather than reactive?

The mistake most people make is to assume that life and money will remain for the rest of their lives when they get it, so they ignore any sort of advice to invest and take care of their money. Sometimes, your best friends are not necessarily found when you become rich, unless they are rich and don't want anything from you. Some people only come into your life because of what you have, and they seek how best to accrue their wealth through you as quickly as they can, and before you know it, it's too late.

Some are there for the right reasons though, and it is great to give back, but while you give, create a tunnel where your well is always filled so you can do more. Also, when some people get to the top, their ego shadows everything else because they don't listen to anyone; power blinds them so much so that by the time they realize it, they are all alone. Remember your career may not always be there, so while you invest, invest also in people. Invest as well in other secured tangible assets while you manage your expenditures.

CHAPTER 9

Know Who You Surrounding Yourself With

Surrounding yourself with the right people does not suggest neglecting others who may not fit the list. While you look up to others higher than you, people beneath you invariably are also looking up to you, so you need to live up to expectation. All the same, make good friends because friends can make or break you. A friend can have a greater influence on your life than you think. In fact, they play a bigger role in your life than your parents, siblings, or close family in most cases. Look at it from this angle: about fifty-five percent of your time is spent outside the home, twenty-five percent is spent at home (but without parents or guardians because they are out working in most cases), and the remaining twenty percent is spent with family. How much influence can your family impact on you with that remaining percent? Even the twenty percent is spent on eating, sleeping, being on the phone, cleaning the house, and all sorts of other sidetrack events, so in actual fact, only about five percent of that time is utilized in quality time with your family. Borrowing the 80/20 rule, if a family is well disciplined, it can engrave good influence on you and direct you with that twenty percent to control the eighty percent, depending on one's family structure.

Note though, that we have different types of friends in life; some become more than families while some are described as 'pain in the neck'. Your duty is, if you can, to identify the difference and manage it. You also need to know what type of friends you need around you to push you towards success. You cannot desire to be a scientist but have artists comprising the greater percentage of all of your friendships. That wouldn't work very well in your life.

Here's a list of different types of friends and some suggested ways to manage, relate and create good relationships with them.

Conversational friends: These are friends that when you meet, all you do is talk about life in general terms, gossip, analyze a situation, or discuss something prevailing and then end it there. You only meet to ignite something new or continue with the previous conversation, and you don't necessarily look for each other for other reasons. You just enjoy each other's conversation and presence and then call it a day. With such people, if you can, speak less and listen more because they could put you into trouble. They are those who seek information, distort the information, filter it, and present it back to you in a form that may or may not be accurate. There are certainly good and excellent conversations that may erupt, but generally, if you read between the lines, most of them are gossips, which you should avoid, so if you meet, speak less by smiling and chip in if necessary. Very soon, you may be a boring friend and may not be sought after again.

Nostalgic friends: Sometimes also referred to as Occasional friends. These are friends similar to conversational friends; however, they are those whom you meet only on specific occasions. Usually, one thing you have in common is the meeting ground. The fact that you meet at that point means you share something in common—it could be in knowledge, a common friend, children, hobby, and the like. These friends prefer to engage you in conversations that remind you of the past and what went on since last time, so to bridge the gap. Depending on where you meet, make sure to gather your thoughts carefully and articulate your words well. For example, if you meet on business grounds, you may be sitting at the same table, and obviously, you cannot avoid them. Engage in conversation but with fewer words, sound interesting and clear. These types of friends usually laugh a lot and share quick jokes and move on to something else afterward. If you meet on a social ground, however, the rhythm may be different. In this instance, you may want to be a little loose, friendlier, but make sure you listen more than you speak. Ask good questions, enjoy each other's company, but remember that's probably it until there is another similar event. Watch what you share, as it might come back to bite you. Conversation should be less formal, less calculated and very informal generally with this type of grouping.

Academic friends: These are friends with whom you meet and talk only about academic stuff. Mostly, these are intellectuals who are also forward-looking people in life. They want to know next steps, researches conducted, books read, lessons learned, where they agree and where they disagree, and comradeship they possess on general viewpoints. They sometimes engage in beneficial arguments and discuss schools that are doing well and not. They discuss investment issues, the new things on the stock market, friends that are in higher positions that they are affiliated with, and their own career. They also talk about global news, speeches made by powerful people, the impact they are making, and 'foolish' decisions by some leaders that are affecting progress to their mutual understanding. With these types of friends, if you are not in that category, you will be misplaced and bored. Nothing of theirs will amuse you because while you are thinking of soap opera and entertainment, they are discussing crypto-currency. You will need to be knowledgeable to fit in here or risk looking like a 'jerk' in front of them. To keep a meaning full relationship you need to be learned and up to speed. It starts with a deep understanding in one and then mastering the next.

They love to engage in positive conversations mostly, compete on current issues, and analyze the result vis-à-vis what you have learned. In this type of friendship, you cannot be quiet; you need to be engaging and contributing strategically all the time.

While this is building your knowledge base, the caution though is to believe in yourself and your values so that some advising you to ignore everything at the expense of building academic know-how does not sway you. Some of them may be suffering in their marriages or just be in cohabitating relationships because they may not have time for anything else. That too isn't bad, however, do what is best for you and do not lay down or compromise on your principles. Some in this group may have an imbalance of life, since their life may be saturated with only academic stuff. The choice is yours to determine at what length to absorb what and also what length to engage.

Spiritual friends: These friends relate to you only on a spiritual basis. They talk spiritual matters and like to pray for each other. They may have different beliefs but share a common spiritual concern. It is a good thing to have spiritual friends, but be careful not to engage in unnecessary arguments, especially when you both belong to different faith groups. Note the difference, you can both be spiritual but belong to different religious groups. You can attempt to win others to your side, but it needs to be done with tact and insight. People could lose friendships easily because of petty-petty issues. You may find common ground, but since each faith group considers itself to be superior over others, one needs to be careful in these areas. Respect each other's religion and probably wait for the right moment to make a move of asking invitation to your side, but be ready to visit theirs too.

Church friends: Unlike the spiritual friends, though still spiritual, church friends usually belong to the same church denomination and share the same belief. Conversations here are usually geared towards the same direction. There is a sense of trust here, though yet to be tested. People change when discussions are outside church discussions. These types of friends only talk about church stuff, things of God, church meetings, Bible verses, and the preacher. While they talk about church programs, pastors, and their leaders, they also focus on preaching methods and then compare their impact and future programs.

You may work with a church friend at work and all they want to do is talk church, and belief and lose sight of the purpose of being at work - which is to work. Of course, if they are in need of counseling or encouragement and you can do it privately do so - but work is work and church is church, if you are witnessing with your life then your example will speak not your words alone. You were not hired to be the preacher, so do your work and focus. You can only survive in this world when you are crafty, strategic, and poised. Some Bible scholars may say not being open about the things of God, means being ashamed of God. I hope I don't get calls on this. That is not my intended meaning. The same Bible advises on being smart and giving to God what belong to God, and to Caesar what belongs to Caesar. Find a better time to witness about your faith, maybe during lunch breaks, during workout sessions, but not when you are expected to perform on the job. If you do the opposite, you rather do not glorify the God you claim to be serving.

Political friends: These are people who connect mainly to discuss political affairs. This could be people who are at the echelon of political heights or aspiring politician friends who just love to talk about politics. It took me years upon years to start paying attention to political issues because I just did not love it. Now I do. I want to know what is happening out there, what our leaders are thinking and doing, what they are using our tax money for, and who to vote for or not. A lot of people disagree with this, but remember, even the word "politics" and its actions are seen everywhere we find ourselves. At the workplace, among friends, in the schools, at discussion tables, at home, on the street and what have you, it is everywhere, anywhere and always. While people genuinely appreciate getting to mingle with people from different cultures, others have to painfully adjust to accept it because they have no choice; they need to play the political game either so to keep their jobs or not to be seen as racist. In other words, politics is everywhere.

It is always advisable not to discuss anything of politics, religion, or relationships in a business setting. These are controversial topics that could derail people from achieving a simple goal. Know the right setting to discuss such topics, and it should be with friends whom you are comfortable with.

Neighborhood friends: Friends in this category only become your friends by the fact that they live close to you physically. I know this may not apply to some people because they live in ranches, big houses, and places distant from their next-door neighbor, but for the average person, they are able to at least see the next house as not too far from each other, even if there is a big wall between them. In some cases, the fact that they meet each other in their common clubhouse is enough to qualify them as neighbors. They are able to discuss issues of common concern affecting the neighborhood, like garbage fees and why the trucks aren't showing up on time, the untidy lawns, complex management-related issues, and playgrounds in other places nicer than theirs, and other fancy stuff that you can think of. These types of friends may be less harmful, but these days, it depends. The world has changed so much that my current neighbor who used to be a marine cried that, in the past, they used to leave their houses unlocked for weeks, but no more. While they try to look after each other, not all have the same sentiment of protection. The world has become so unsafe and unpredictable that, one has to be extra sure in order to entertain trust. Currently, trust has become the priciest commodity in this world, and it is no different from those who live close to each other.

Just because they are your neighbors doesn't mean they should know everything about you. Be careful who you call your best friend. These are friends you can't avoid so much because you meet them when getting out of your garage, when dropping your children from school, when you take a walk or go on an exercise run. It is inevitably good to live in peace with your neighbors, even if they are not your friends.

Club friends: It is jokingly said that when you marry a person you met at a club, you shouldn't be surprised when you always find your spouse in the club. A past military lecturer friend of mine once said you will never see him holding an alcoholic drink in any picture. The reason is simple; you never know where that picture may end up, who will see it, or what it may be used for. The fear is, it may be used against you tomorrow. I know of many friends who go to the club but do not drink alcohol, however, only a few people fall under that category. Nonetheless, avoid serious discussions in the club. When the music is going and your body is moving to the rhythm of the music, and the other hand is holding a glass of 'something', nothing serious goes into that brain anymore. Don't waste your time.

Simply put, when you drink and have no control over your mouth, just avoid talking altogether. You will embarrass yourself the next day. Even if you don't drink, the other person(s) may not be like you. Do not follow friends who are ordering for more glasses of wine or more bottles of what they love, their energy and experience may be way further from yours. Some of you, all you need is to smell the scent of the drink and you're done. Especially ladies, watch out. Your hormones are tested and aroused much quicker and things you may not have wished to happen would. Where you meet someone, including the club doesn't matter, you can create the best out of it, as has been the case for many.

Work-related friends: They are the ones whom you only meet at work, conduct business, and that's it! They usually don't have any other relationship and/or connection to you once they leave the work environment. Some do, but not many. These types of friends share issues that affect their work, jokes about work, sometimes talk about their weekend activities, or gossip about their bosses or subordinates, depending on which aisle they are in. With such friends, keep work conversation separate from private conversation. Some people transition this into personal friendship; however, once a colleague is transferred or leaves for another company, the relationship often fades or ceases to exist as normal. This is why this type of friendship is regarded as work-related. Be cautious about what you share and discuss. Sometimes, people will want to dig into your brain to know what is there, so it is up to you to determine the level of conversation to engage in. The same people can make or unmake you; they may also do things that seem like they favor you (yes, sometimes it is genuine), but no one loves you like you do. I have met the good, bad, and ugly, and inner connections will tell you who is genuine and who isn't. I have made some mistakes, which shouldn't happen to anyone. Do not discuss private issues at work, and as one great man whom I respect advised, focus on work and do not let anyone assume you're drifting

Friends who take and those who give: Regardless of any of the types and ranges of friends described, we have two interesting types of friends that you can find anywhere on this planet: the takers and givers. Friends who take are those who always need something from you but never seem to give anything in return. They will do anything to get what they want from you through fair and foul means. They are dangerous. Such friends will not bring any value to your life.

On the other hand, we have friends who just give and give without expecting anything in return. Be careful not to confuse receiving such gifts to mean all of a sudden you have a friend. Because most people live with needs, they affiliate generosity to mean friendship. The same way they offer you whatever it is that you need, so they do for others, and you're no exception.

Do not take advantage of someone who showed you mercy at a point of need. Consider what you too can do to return the favor if possible, and do not run into their arms every day. You can become a nuisance over time.

Balanced friends (give and take): We have friends who take but at the same time give as well. They are neither hoarders nor selfish. They meet and share, they give help when another friend is in need, and they expect to be helped when they are in need. This type of friendship is usually healthy and long-lasting. Helping each other does not mean you measure at the same level, but you both have a sense of commitment. Once when I was young I was given a nice shirt from a rich person. I went for the parcel with a token gift of a box of orange juice as a gift in return. An orange juice with a shirt? What a total mismatch! But due to the fact that I made an effort of a give and take, I maintained a high level of respect with this man over a long period of time.

I give back to my alma mater and many institutions through resume reviews, lecturing, board membership, and/or coaching students to be prepared for the world ahead of them. I do all of these with great passion and dedication because I am blessed with what the world has given offered me, and it is time to give back.

Friends who are Mentors or Tormentors: We usually define mentors as people in higher positions, more qualified than us, and older than we are. Wisdom is mostly associated with grey hair as well, but this is not always the case. Obviously, there is no mistake to take advice from someone who has the fruit on the tree, no question about that, but not everyone with grey hair is wise. I have been and continue to be a mentor to people who were above me in certain areas. Friends can serve as each other's mentors. I have a friend who always teases me that I speak like a sixty-year-old man when I advise people.

Do not despise anyone in your circle. Mentors who are friends may be experts in a particular field where they provide superior knowledge to guide you in order to sail through what you need at a particular time. Learn as much knowledge as you need from such people. I believe in exponential knowledge, and also that no one person knows it all. It is better to listen to the full spread when someone is making a point than to conclude too early—what you think you know may not be enough to propel you to the top. When mentors or people of such knowledge speak, it is like providing you with data. What we know about data is that it is raw in nature and unprocessed. It is up to you to process all that you have heard from different experts and turn it into your information. Find mentors that practice what they preach to you.

Tormentors, on the other hand, are friends who seek any possible means to discourage you. They always don't come as tormentors at the initial stages; they may initially come with good motives. Others have ulterior motives from the beginning. If possible, stay away from these people.

Sports/Entertainment friends: Who doesn't want this? Because I engage in sports, I can relate to how easily one can make friends in this area. It becomes easier for these people to get connected because they share a common purpose, a common goal, a common destiny, and a common passion. This applies to any friendship segment, be it dancing groups, political groups, or what have you.

It is advisable to keep in close contact with your sports team, share ideas, receive ideas, and always work as a team. You may have people within the group that you may trust, especially previous experts to learn from, in the areas of any mistakes and how not to repeat those mistakes.

Seasonal friends: Similar to occasional friends, but these are friends whom you meet within a particular era or cycle in your life and may never meet again. Even if you do, you rarely have anything to say or discuss. This usually occurs mostly with roommates, at conferences, seminars, fundraising ceremonies, a difficult time in life, a joyous time in life, on a vacation, on a short project, and the like. Have you ever experienced this? Do you remember a time that you met someone during a cruise and became excellent friends thinking it would last, only to separate for a while, and immediately the interest also fades? Some are lucky though, but not many.

These are seasonal friends. When was the last time you met with some of your old schoolmates? And I don't mean on social media. The answer is likely either never or some time ago, unless during reunions or you form a particular bond of friendship with a few of them. You occasionally meet and have fun, and the next time you meet that person again, you are talking about stories from ten years ago or catching up over what has happened since the last time you met up.

The point is, these types of seasonal friends are fun when you meet them for a short time, but unless there is a special bond, make it short-lived and fun.

Friends who form a combination: You may have a certain type of friend who possesses a combination of some of the above elements. They are less boring because of the fact that they have a lot to talk about. Sometimes you need people like this to make your day. They may be positive or negative, depending on the topic; however, you will mostly enjoy their company when you share the same sentiments with them. For example, your conversation with this friend can span sports, academic, religion, business - to other topics of commonality. With this friend the conversations just flow - like wine at a wedding. This way, you continue to engage in dialogues that are mutually enjoyable and potentially mutually beneficial.

All-round friends: They are usually your best friend. This is someone you can confide in. You both can share issues relating to religion, work (though you may be working in different industries), sports, relationships, marriage, and all issues of common interest. Even when your friend does not have a child, for example, but you do, you both can easily discuss any topic freely without calculating your words. You would hardly feel tired or bored with such friends because every topic on the table is of interest. The danger though is that you may tend to spend a lot of time with such friends— sometimes more than your family—because this type of friend becomes like family, unless discussions are homely, if you're married, for example. This type of friend is probably the most influential. As parents, this is the type of people you will like to know because they influence your child. There is an adage that says, "If you want to know me, take a look at my friends."

FOOD FOR THOUGHT:

We have all kinds of friends out there, but the key point is whatever group or groups you fall in, they are all trying to find a safe place that fits their place of comfort.

What kind of a friend are you? Where do you fall? You may be a best friend to someone but just a work-related friend to another. You may be a club friend to one person, but someone else knows you only as a sports contributor because all you both talk about when you meet is sports and nothing else. Above all, you may be an all-around friend to someone, but that person may not regard you as part of his or her all-around friend network. It is an interesting world we live in, and the earlier you start accepting certain facts and begin adjusting to it, the better it will be for you eventually. Life is too short to spend it with the wrong people. Friends should be people you can trust and rely on.

KNOW WHO YOU SURROUNDING YOURSELF WITH

Let your 'Maker' choose your friends for you. Listen to good advice from people who have been successful through the storms of life. The majority of friendships fall apart over time, but those that stand the test of time are worth nurturing. Other so-called friends will show you their true colors when something goes wrong, and you won't like what you see. Learning from the situation will save you from taking the wrong path.

I have been blessed with some good friends in life, people who were there for me and who still are and vice versa, people who believed in me when others didn't, people who stood by me in times of difficulty, people who do not discriminate based on religion. not of the same faith. I had friends who provided and cared for me when needed, visited me when I was lonely, and shared encouragement.

Nevertheless, there are people who pretend to be friends but who would gladly turn on you in a second if it would benefit them. Don't cry. A superpower may be laying another opportunity for you by naturally eliminating those people from your path. They may not be bad people, in fact, most aren't, just that, the gel is finished. See that train off!!!

CHAPTER 10

Do Not Eat Your Seeds—Plant Them

According to the law of nature, the ant saves up for the winter so he can have food and warmth, if he doesn't - he would not survive the winter. The bear fattens up before hibernation, if not he may not make it through the winter, and so, the wealthy person had to learn the lesson and discipline of saving and investing and therefore able to maintain or grow his or her wealth for a rainy day.

Before delving into the nitty-gritty of what needs to be done, there is the need to take a quick pause and get some explanations right.

First and foremost, not many people have been exposed to or been privileged to know what the metaphor of fruits and or seeds mean. However, there are some who have been.

Whatever your case may be, this chapter is here to assist you by opening your eyes deeper, and, if possible, to some extent, gear you towards being proactive so as to avoid the mistakes that may cost you dearly.

Some people may feel its too late because they made a bad financial decision and are so buried in debt they can't envision how to reverse it. This chapter will guide you into taking the appropriate steps to regain your freedom. Its never too late as long as you have the will.

How do you separate the seeds from the fruit in the first place? How do you identify and differentiate them? This should be the first step, which calls for vision, direction, and focus. This calls for delayed gratification as opposed to instant gratification.

The seed and the fruit are just metaphorical statements describing the best way to live our lives. The seed in this instance refers to opportunities and chances one is presented to, for which one needs to preserve, save or invest into. It's also their decision making and actions. Whereas, the fruit is the build-up of the seed, where you gain and now enjoy from what you had invested into. Let's make one simple analogy out of this; Ethan is given one thousand US dollars ($1,000) by his Uncle William during a surprise visit to their house. Ethan was not expecting this money, and did not need it in the short run. And so, he, being wise, saw the money as a seed, and so sought the advice of an investment expert, who invested it in a secured investment pool. In about five years when Ethan needs it most, the accumulated interest was ten thousand US dollars ($10,000 USD), which becomes a fruit for him now. At this point, Ethan will be much better financially than his friend Brandon who was in the same condition, however, used his money five years earlier to buy clothes that he didn't actually need.

Many people are living social media lives and pretending to be something they aren't. It is only the unwise that says tomorrow is unknown so let's rejoice and spend everything we have today—after all, who cares, life is short!

It may be short, but it tends to be long for you when you are in the clutches of sorrow. It is only fools that spend all they have in a day, never thinking about tomorrow. Some people want to enjoy all they have right now because they have good jobs right now, they are well paid today, they have the network, and their cash flow seems to be constantly flowing. So why don't they spend it when it comes? Unwise!

Listen; we all have certain moments in our lives when we want to splurge. That is different. Even then, splurge wisely, and always remember someone somewhere needs your help to survive. Love yourself, and by all means, do not deprive yourself of good and beautiful things. After all, that is why you're working and living, but remember tomorrow as well while you spend today.

There are some blessings that come our way, for which one should be generous with reinvestment. I know of people who take advantage of other people's wealth selfishly. Such people are parasites and not in this bracket. Rather, I am referring to people who genuinely need your help.

God places people in your life for a reason, and you're also placed in other people's lives for a reason as well. Life is lived once and must be treated with respect, joy, and careful planning for success.

Many were the rich folks who lived on millions of dollars, but because they lacked wisdom and were 'deaf' to good advice, they lost their wealth in the wind, as described earlier.

Lack of wisdom and mismanagement is tantamount to eating your seed.

Sometimes it depends on how one got one's riches. If you earn it and really suffer for it, you will appreciate how to manage it because you have been there before. And don't forget your roots, friends and family who were there for you when you needed it most. Aunties like Gladys, uncle's like Enoch (Yayra), sisters, cousins, parents, godparents like Abe, distant relatives, and people who prayed for and supported you in diverse ways like Emmanuel, should not be neglected when things get better for you. Learn to give back and know that you can only give back when you have it, and also know that you can only give more back when you have more. Learn to plant the seeds in your life rather than eat them now.

FOOD FOR THOUGHT:

Patience is key here. This fast and ever-changing environment we have found ourselves in comes with its blessings and challenges. Many people want quick and easy money to better their lifestyle, and they do not have the necessary patience to learn and grow as professionals to be able to appreciate what they have. People are living competitive lives that aren't helping them in any way, but they do it anyway to please others. My suggestion is to take your time, identify what is good for you, seek good advice, and surround yourself with people who are wiser, better, and who want to help you progress in life. Life and happiness are not measured in only financial gains or riches, but in wealth.

To me, wealth is defined by the time I get to do what I want, when I want it and how I want it. The type of friend's and the impact you have on their lives and vice versa also defines it. It also includes riches, good health, great family, excellent friends, making a mark in people's lives, eating healthy, putting smiles on other people's faces, knowing the difference between the seed and the fruit, when to plant what and when to eat what, and indeed applying this knowledge to become a fruit.

In the kingdom of the forest, regardless of the economy in the forest, the lion has to hide from and then outrun its prey to survive. While a predator becomes prey to one, that predator is also prey to another because they depend on each other to survive. Wwe live in an echo system. Only the strongest, smartest, fastest, and the wisest survive the economy of the jungle. If animals are that wise, why not human beings?

Consider the ant that gathers its food while most others rely on a daily meal. They spend large amounts of time together to store as much food as possible when it is available, and so when it is their dry season, they cross their legs and enjoy. Others rely on the misleading notion that the food would always be there, so let's enjoy it all today and forget about tomorrow because tomorrow will take care of itself.

The ant doesn't think that way. It is always thinking about separating the seed from the fruit, so they will eat what they need to survive on today to get them the energy to work hard for tomorrow when it is all gone. Let us learn from the wisdom of the ant and not just know what to do but actually put it into practice.

CHAPTER 11

Learning to Be Content with What You Have

Being content doesn't mean remaining stuck where you are. Rather, be happy where you are today because you are alive and have opportunities.

I've come to understand also that the reason a lot of people aren't content or happy with what they have or do in life is the fact that they do not have the calling for what they do. They may be paid well in the profession they are in, but waking up to perform their duties becomes a chore rather than joy. Complaints, nagging, grumbling, negative gossip will take you nowhere. As indicated, people mistake contentment for settlement. There is a big difference. Life is too short to spend half of it in distress. Being content is not a suggestion that you shouldn't pursue your dreams; however, you have to be appreciative of who you are, how far you've come, and what you are capable of achieving.

According to economic theory, human needs are insatiable and will never be satisfied on face value. The more you have, the more you need.

Consider someone who is dying of hunger. The first and most important need of that person at that moment is not sitting in a mansion or riding firstclass in an airplane or driving the best car. Nope, it is food. Nothing matters more at that moment. Once they have food, they can begin to think about other wants and needs. It is all about chasing satisfaction first and the quest to gratify gastric demands deadens one's tastes in the meantime, but when satisfaction begins to set in, the faults in the food would begin to pop up— too salty, too much pepper, too cold, etc.

My wife and I have taken care of many people whom we picked from nowhere and brought into our house to support us and be paid in return for their service. We went the extra mile by sending some to school to give them hope, not mentioning the love we provided to them. We allowed them to have access to everything that we had so that they feel completely part of the family. But when they started seeing things in a different light after being exposed to a different lifestyle—yes, because first and foremost, food and clothing were no longer the issue they used to be—these same people almost immediately forgot who they had been and then started comparing themselves to what they thought they deserved to be rather than appreciating the difference between where they had come from and where they were.

They started comparing themselves to our children, so much so that, now, getting them to clean and wash and do what they were paid for, became a headache. They started misbehaving, dressing more than the madam of the house. Dusting the house was seen as a big chore and bother, something that was the initial reason for which they had come in as stated. Sometimes, some get confused over who the boss of the house, obviously not me, because we try to create an environment free to all. This is not against someone who looks good and desires to dress. We are rather advocates of looking good and creating a good personal brand for people, especially those who serve. If you treat them bad, it will be obvious for people to see who you are and it will be a reflection on you, so we are particular about that. The point is how unappreciative some could be after you show them kindness.

I recall when one such young lady came to our house, and for the first couple of weeks, was experiencing bouts of stomachache! We were worried most of the time, only to determine later her sickness was due to the change of food and eating habits. She was going almost a day without food when she was not with us; then, all of a sudden, she was exposed to three times daily meals and snacks. She was overeating, which caused her stomachaches. This continued until she got stabilized. Upon realizing the cause, we had to assure her that the food was not going anywhere, and that as long as she stayed with us, food would not be a problem. Unfortunately, she was among those who saw life suddenly differently after a while. Sad!

At a very young age I moved in with an aunty to attend a prestigious school at the time. This aunty of mine was a trader and so baked bread and sold groceries to the community where we lived. She was so kind to me during my two year stay with her in every aspect. As a result of what she did, I learned the process of baking and helping her sell her groceries. I wasn't a perfect child by any means, but I always attempted to support her, even at that age. I knew my parents didn't necessarily give her daily provisions to take care of me, but I never saw her complain about me. I kept a good relationship with her till I completed that part of my education and left to join my siblings in the big city. I recall thinking so much about her, mostly because she never had a child of her own but took care of many other relatives. When I had the opportunity and met her after so many years later, I gave her everything in my pocket without a blink. It was a spiritual moment for me, though I could not pay her back for everything she did for me. At least, I showed gratefulness and she was overly excited to see me as a son.

I know of people who are never satisfied with whatever they have. They will nag and nag and nag until they get to the next stage. You'd think when they got to the destination of their dreams, they would be satisfied, but nope. They would recycle the same attitude over and over again and fail to appreciate life for what it brings.

Sometimes, is it is good to take a break, look around you, compare yourself with those who look up to you, appreciate how far you've come, and then appreciate life.

Take a little time out, enjoy life a bit, and move on. Research reveals that human beings on the average spend about forty percent of their life sleeping, and to put it in numerical terms, if you're currently thirty years old, then you have already spent about twelve years out of those years sleeping. Wow! Imagine adding your complain time. Oh boy, you're not just wasting time, you're losing it against yourself. It is better to spend some of your precious time on ventures that would benefit you. One way or the other, everyone complains at some point, and there is nothing wrong with that in principle, but when you make it a daily habit, then there is a problem.

SYNERGY AND COMMONALITY

I have always told people who are close to me that, on a travel map, there are resting points, and they are created naturally for a reason for survival. So please, take some time in your life to pause, appreciate life, and enjoy it before it passes by.

While you may be envious of someone, little do you know what type of issues those whom you wish to be are facing. Some may be driving the best and most expensive cars, traveling all over the world, wearing the best dresses and jewelry, and eating at the most expensive restaurants, but they may also be going through a serious illness and have a limited amount of time left. You never know.

There is nothing wrong in wishing to be like anyone but my observation is, while you wish to be like them, silently, others are also hoping to be like you, so then, why not wish to be you but a better you because you're unique?

In his words, Bonnie Dean quoted Nelson Mandela as saying, "*It is what we make out of what we have, not what we are given, that separates one person from another.*"

Wealth, comes in the form of healthy living, good family, the ability to get out of bed and put your feet on the ground every day, having a peaceful relationship and many more. Riches, on the other hand, comes in the form of physical money, and because these two terms are not clearly defined, it opens the door for confusion and internal mental chaos. In all you do, be careful where you talk and what you talk about because you never know who is connected to whom. The world is like a decision tree where someone somewhere is connected to one another.

Just because someone works for you does not mean you automatically have that person's trust. You need to earn that trust. Do not confuse someone kneeling before you to mean the person is humble and sober, and so, thinking you own the person. Big mistake. That person is just protecting his or her meal in the time being.

Someone may be kneeling before you but standing in their hearts, while others may be standing before you but may be kneeling with humility in their minds and hearts.

Don't get bogged down with the cultural acrobatics that people are enslaved with all over the world. Depending on where you come from, learn to acknowledge other people's opinion and respect them even if you don't agree with them.

FOOD FOR THOUGHT:

Learn to appreciate each day as they come. Think about the fact that it is Monday, but it doesn't mean the next Monday will be the same. Your age will not be the same. The composition of the world and what is happening at the time will change. The weather may be different. You may receive fewer phone calls than the previous Monday. The statistics of people who may perish that day or during the week may be totally different from the previous one. The demands of the day are nothing compared to the previous one. The point is simple. Take some time off, open your window, see the light outside, the sun, and the moon, savor, and enjoy the sight.

I have made it a point to do the following as a family whenever we could. Raising three boys is not easy, so we have determined to sometimes take turns taking time off. I might take a weekend here and there to go somewhere special, relax, and not think about the dishes, vacuuming, or picking up anyone from any place. Then my wife takes her turn, doing the same thing. Then, we take a turn relaxing somewhere as a family. This is where we mostly travel outside the country or visit a special place locally purposely for the enjoyment of the children and the entire family while we adapt.

We sometimes also have movie nights for the children, and just as it is in the airplane when we travel, the entire row of five at the movie theatre is taken at a movie center for relaxation. I never knew I would love kids' movies until I had kids. I am now the champion patron.

CHAPTER 12

Diverse Talents

We are all uniquely talented. We all have been gifted with special talents, but the reason many people struggle may be lack of opportunities or the fact that they still haven't found their strings for the right music as yet.

People are still looking for the right pitch for their match while others still haven't found their gloves for the snow. Consider the story of Dolores Huerta, who was an activist for the Hispanic community and the minority in the 1960s. Although she wanted to be a dancer, she later became a human rights activist, due to the oppression her people were going through. She sacrificed her entire life fighting for the destitute and the voiceless just as Martin Luther King Jr. did. She had eleven children from three marriages and was mostly away from her children. At one point she did not know which high school one of her sons was attending until after eight months. She was beaten, bruised, and tortured, but she did not give up on her goal. Dolores inspired President Obama when he came up with his campaign slogan *"Yes We Can"* for his 2008 U.S presidential bid. Her slogan had been *"Si Se Puede,"* meaning *"Yes We Can."* She sacrificed her comfort and personal life fighting for humanity, according to her legendary documentary. Her sole mission was to see people become free, especially her native Hispanics.

Though she did not pursue her initial dancing career, to many, she danced with her voice throughout her life. Same it is with all who paid a dear price by sacrificing something of theirs for others.

Nonetheless, we all have our unique and gifted talents in life, and everyone has a role to play to complete the special puzzle that is naturally created. Just as the body parts also have their different roles, so are all made to perform their duties to their utmost ability. The ear, for example, is meant to hear and listen, not to walk. And the stomach is meant to digest food, not to breathe. Each part contributes to the body's movement to complete its role in forming a normal functioning human being.

Not all of us are born to become athletes. Not everyone can be an entrepreneur. It is important to identify your goal as early as possible. Even if you identify it later in life, it is better than not finding your path. The eye cannot be the ear. If the leg tells the arm, *"I wish to be like you,"* the arm has its own function and was created uniquely for that purpose. Black, White, Indian, Hindu, Christian, Muslim, or whatever, we must all work together with our talents to make the world a better place. There are many people who are in the wrong jobs or who are heading in the wrong direction.

Sometimes, you may be right but also wrong. You may be doing the right thing the wrong way. Usually, it is not the person but the skill set that does not match the job's expectation. You may be right in choosing the right career path but may be wrong in choosing an organization that does not fit. When this happens, people tend to think that something is wrong with their career as a whole. It may be time to rediscover, rethink, and get some coaching and direction to make the perfect life-changing decision. Apples and oranges are two separate fruits. You cannot wish to be both. Learn to know what you desire for in life.

Consider this scenario as an example: Evans Jr. (SJ) and his brother Eamonn were fighting over a piece of orange they bought. They fought and cried over the orange until someone came to their rescue to help them divide it. There was peace, and so they both went their separate ways. When SJ got home, he immediately took out the seed and planted it for a future orange tree and more oranges. He didn't need any other thing, and so, threw rest away. When Eamonn also got home, he took out the seeds, which he didn't need, peeled off the skin, and used the skin of the orange for medicine. What a waste? If they both had just sat down to determine what they truly wanted in the orange, there could have had peace for which they didn't have to fight. They both could have just had enough of what they wanted, and they would have benefitted much better from that orange.

Do not wish to be someone else, but you can desire to perform like that person and better. There are some who may seem successful, but inwardly they have issues you wouldn't want to know.

Note:

Not all are born to do certain things; identify your passion and pursue it with respect, diligence, and commitment as though that was your last chance.

When you make a name for yourself and you have both the reputation and integrity, everything you say is regarded as correct. Even if it doesn't make sense, people find wisdom in it. Integrity and reputation may be closely related, but there is a slight difference. While reputation is how one positions oneself to be recognized or perceived in the public or private domain, integrity, on the other hand, is doing what you say you want to. It is about practicing what you preach. One can have reputation but not integrity, but it is difficult to have integrity without reputation.

Talking of reputation and integrity, I have had experiences in situations where people at the bottom of the organization's ladder may suggest an idea which is not taken—not even considered, in fact, not even heard—but within a few months, when the same idea is presented by a senior Executive, the whole organization embraces it like a fresh idea.

One of the biggest wastes is a good idea that is not considered early. We shouldn't forget the fact that fresh and innovative ideas sometimes come from the bottom. Ignoring such ideas may cause some roadblocks for whichever organization it is in the future. Not all ideas are good; however, the worst position is not to consider them at all.

THE SIX BLIND MEN:

There is an interesting story about the six blind folks and the elephant. The story goes this way: They were blind from birth, so obviously they had never seen anything before, let alone an elephant. One day, they decided to feel around a live elephant to determine how it looked like.

The first person declared that an elephant was like wall. Why? He had fallen against the broadside of the elephant and felt his hand around it. The second, laughed and asserted that an elephant couldn't be like a wall. Rather, it was like a tree, just because he was only able to hold its leg, and so how could it be like a wall? The third blind man laughed at the two friends and professed an elephant was like a fan because he had held its big open ears, which were flapping. The fourth said, *"guys, you're crazy."* He was sad to realize how blind indeed the rest were, and he wanted to let them know what crazy stuff they were talking about. To him, an elephant was like a rope because he had held the tail. The fifth, at this time, was extremely angry because he had held the tusk of the elephant. He burst out saying an elephant was like a spear. At this time, the sixth blind person was fuming as he insisted that an elephant was like a big rough stone. Why? Because this one had held its head. It wasn't long until a seeing person, Emmanuel, a.k.a Swizer, came onto the scene and asked what the issues were. When he was told the story and why they were fighting each other, he buried his head in his hands. Each of the six blind people was eager to know the verdict, believing he was right in his own way, based on their senses and what they had individually experienced. They demanded to know the verdict, and to their disappointment and surprise, Swizer carefully sat them down and told them that each one of them had a piece of the truth. If they combined all that they each had held and described, they would have had a full elephant.

They were stunned and felt stupid. At least, it was a big lesson for them to learn to listen to each other going forward, especially regarding things they hadn't experienced in their life before.

The issue with some of us is that we see things from only one angle and then draw immediate conclusions. We see people of a different race and then immediately assume they are poor or do not have common sense. We see refugees and assume because they don't speak our language, they may be 'beasts'. If we had the ability to determine from birth which tribe, region, family, and/or country to come from, we all would have ridden on white horses. We are not prepared to listen to one another's viewpoint, or even consider it. We need to understand that our talents are unique and special, no one person knows everything, and that is why the rule of synergy and commonality is stronger than one. It is imperative to identify talents and place the right talent in the right job. Some talents are also not properly utilized because those possessing them do not have the opportunity to speak, and even if they do, no one listens. That is why you need to earn your reputation in whatever you do, and make sure you do it well to your utmost best.

DIVERSE TALENTS

I know of people who did well in their previous roles, but when that responsibility changed, their performance dropped drastically, leading to their failure and disgrace. I know also of people who overstayed their leadership welcome but refused to identify the wisdom to say goodbye.

FOOD FOR THOUGHT:

While you think you know it all, someone knows better than you. The claps of yesterday for your achievements do not constitute future claps, so instead of relying on yourself to prepare the ground, play the drum, do the dance and be the cheerleader at the same time, why not get others involved? Your eyes can only see so much; it could take someone to help you see better. When you are drawing a straight line, without anyone behind you guiding and advising on how to pave it, you might end up with a crooked line.

It is vital to consider other people's opinions and respect them even if you don't like them. If you don't, you may end up jumping well but landing on the wrong foot.

✶ ✶ ✶

CHAPTER 13

Wastes in Life and in Business, and Second Chances

Waste is anything that is technically not wanted. When you eliminate waste, quality improves while production time and costs are reduced drastically.

Part of the keys in which we don't succeed in life has to do with not adhering to simple rules. Some of such symptoms include; procrastination, bad decision, fearing to fail, distractions, lost opportunities, delays, indecision, waiting, not respecting time, inefficient use of resources like overspending, and worse of all, mistaking movement to mean success. This is because you can be seen moving but not adding value to your life.

The above is not different from wastes in business environments. Some of the terms may differ or similar, but there are similarities in terms of its effects and how to deal with them.

When I was on the corporate ladder in my previous life, I was eager to make a difference. My goal was to contribute my part as a unit, under the main agenda for synergistic success. Among many other things, I drove common wastes in production and process management. These wastes could apply to how we live our daily lives as well, which has nothing necessarily to do with manufacturing set-ups nor systems-oriented institutions. Just like the earlier identified wastes in personal life, that of the business is; inappropriate processing, overproduction, overstocking, defects, transportation, excess motion and waiting.

SYNERGY AND COMMONALITY

The above are usually called the seven wastes in the business process.

Upon thorough research and observation, I came across two additional wastes, making them the nine wastes overall, as; unused talent and knowing all of the above eight wastes but doing nothing about them.

The eighth and ninth wastes, as far as I am concerned, are the biggest wastes of all, in terms of process management, operation, manufacturing, and general business management.

Note that, a more detailed explanation of the nine business wastes could be found at the *appendix* of this book with practical examples.

For those who listened, it worked for them. I was doing everything to contribute to the bottom-line as key to corporate success by playing my part well.

It was exciting because the results were real. I was able to acquire my Lean Six Sigma Black Belt in the process, saving millions of dollars as a result. However, it took people, it took synergy and it took collaboration to arrive at any positive result. One cannot do without the other.

Conventional wisdom teaches us that no one is indispensable or irreplaceable based on the above. No matter what you do, note that someone else can do it—and possibly do it better. You become better when you keep on learning, when you read professional newsletters and good books and surround yourself with like-minded people (those with the same commonalities), and listen to wisdom from even those people who are in lower positions. Always bear in mind that subordinates will not always be subordinates. It may be your time and season now, but their time will come, and they will remember all the moments they spent with you. Companies that get overtaken quickly are those that rely on goodwill and past glories, never wanting to improve, ignoring advice on identified waste. I couldn't agree more with Vickie Milano when she said, *"No enterprise is unsinkable, the Titanic sank its first time out. Often it's not hitting the iceberg but fear of hitting it that drowns."* The age of sharing ideas has arrived. The times are beyond mere talk. Knowledge has not just increased; it has exploded, and we need to keep sharing this wisdom for leveraging and synergistic growth. Some people are gifted with unique and smart ideas, but they may not have a clue how to execute those ideas, while others are also gifted at executing those ideas but may not be able to generate the ideas themselves. We need the amalgam of talents to attain lasting success. Do not waste that opportunity.

In the work environment, for example, everyone is needed provided one sets the stage well. Those who dig (research) to get the information are equally needed as those who are excellent at putting the data together. The same goes for those who can yoke the presentation to work together, and those who can present the information succinctly to attract attention.

Some are born naturally shy, who cannot stand in front of the camera or do anything public-related. Such people usually love to work behind the scenes. Sometimes they receive some recognition, but other times they do not. Such people can articulate their viewpoints when you get close to them, but some, though unable to verbally articulate themselves, speak via their actions. Do not despise anyone. You can train people to become what you want them to become, but not everyone can achieve that, so understand them and let the wheel keep rolling. Remember you cannot force the eye to play the ear, neither can you force the leg to perform the arm's duties; it would not be perfect. Just as every part of the body depends on each other to perform their duties to perfection, so is the workplace or whatever environment you find yourself. It takes both subordinates and superiors to work together to make the CEO look good in front of the cameras or with shareholders in order to produce the perfect result. A number of unsung heroes might have worked behind the scenes, some who may never be known, but they contributed to and ensured that success. The analyzers, report creators, the number crunchers, and many more had done their job before someone very important in the group finally presented it. Ignore and look down on one person in the chain, you're just creating waste for which could cost you a lot. At every stage, someone has to be the expert that manages that chain stage, and those people are the best at explaining and articulating each line item and why some insertions are in the document. This is where the principle of synergy works best, where everyone works towards a common goal, thereby creating the sense of harmony within diverse groups.

Just like a hub of a wheel, looking at it from all points on the perimeter of the wheel,

"If you look at each spoke of the wheel independently, it appears to be leading in a different direction from all the others. But that is only because each is starting from a different direction point, and to reach the same endpoint, it has to head in its unique direction that is expected to take it to the "hub" of truth, just as each of us travels a different path to reach the same ultimate truth."

– Pat McKelvey.

FOOD FOR THOUGHT:

When it comes to managing wastes, be it in life or in business, consider mitigating it, avoiding it, reducing it, or best, deleting it if you can.

It takes humility to accept someone's unique perspective. In a basketball or soccer game, someone needs to pass the ball to the scorer to enable a perfect goal. Share the credit. Look out for the right talents, but most importantly, look for people with integrity, credibility, passion, and competence. What benefit do you get in getting only someone with great competence without integrity, and what will you gain in credibility without the necessary competence? Let people feel a part of what they do to encourage them to perform their best every day. Acknowledge greatness; celebrate milestones the same way you easily point out mistakes. Finally, give people second chances in life, not ten chances like people expect. If mistakes continue, do not feel guilty to have a separation with that individual, probably that's not the right place for that one. You may be blessing that person by your decision in disguise. In all these, let discipline be your hallmark. Usually, they are much better than getting new people because they have learned their lessons.

Remember the 89th Oscars in 2017 in the USA, where there was a howler in presenting the "Best Motion Picture" awards?

Warren Beatty and his co-presenter, Faye Dunaway, were given the wrong envelope. They followed the lead in obeying what was in the envelope and mentioned 'La La Land' instead of 'Moonlight'. It was reported that it wasn't their fault; however, everyone assumed they were the ones who'd messed up. It was one of the biggest embarrassments on stage. La La Land crews were already on the stage, starting to speak with joy, shouts, and screams and thanking people with the usual animation. Then, abruptly, someone took the microphone and re-announced the real winner. It was bizarre. Everyone would have thought that was the end of Warren Beatty and his co-presenter Faye Dunaway. However, during the 90th Oscars, in 2018, just the following year after that mishap, they were given a second chance. The exact spot, the last scene, the exact *"Best Most Picture."* They came gallantly and were received with a standing ovation, and when they took the microphone again, they gently made a joke of the entire episode. Then they carefully opened the envelope and made it perfect. This time, 'The Shape of Water' won without any drama. I was on my feet as well in my living hall live on the television. Earlier that day, I had a similar feeling that I wished they would have invited the same couple to come and do that presentation, and to see that happen was surreal. The point is, second chances are important.

I know this for sure: in basketball, when you get a rebound, it's a second chance that gives you another opportunity to score. Do not waste that chance!

CHAPTER 14

Good Leadership

What does *"good leadership"* mean? One evening after returning from the office, I had a thought about leadership and immediately wrote it down. Even though I was exhausted from the day and feeling drowsy, that thought whispered in my brains, and then woke me right up.

The thought was, when you are a leader, you should have followers. If you do not have anyone following you, you are not a leader but rather someone taking a stroll all by yourself.

I was so fascinated by the statement that I regained my waning energy. While that statement sounded funny, it dawned on me that it was true to its core.

A Zambian newspaper article in the early 1990s quoted a statement that described two types of leaders in a simple way: When you are a leader and you have people behind you, they are either following you or chasing after you, depending on your style of leadership.

I will add the third element based on experience: You are probably only being watched from a distance. As a leader, you may be receiving what the Ghanaian military calls *"pamfu"* respect, meaning feigned respect, so do not take every *"yes sir"* to mean you are being heard or are on top of the hill.

No leader is an island; you need people around you to lead. You need to have people who believe in your principles to be a genuine and successful leader. What makes an excellent leader is someone who listens, directs, who is effective and contagious, is intelligent and knows what they are doing, respects their subordinates and colleagues, and practices what they preach.

The qualities of a leader also include being someone who is humble but firm and a visionary. According to the Harvard Business Review on "What Makes a Leader": "*Narcissists have vision, but that's not enough. People in mental hospitals also have visions. The simplest definition of a leader is someone whom other people follow.*" If you desire to satisfy everyone through your leadership, I will advise that you stop deceiving yourself. Whatever you do, not everyone will applaud you.

Ask yourself this question: Why should anyone trust your leadership or agree to follow you?

Technology executive Gilbert Amelio once said, "*If a leader can't get a message across clearly and motivate others to act on it, then having a message doesn't even matter*" (referenced from Communicating Effectively, by Garry Kranz).

This, to me, means a leader must have a voice that is trustworthy, permeable, commands attention, and possesses a sensible message. Leadership doesn't call for always being the one who speaks first and speaks last.

One mistake some leaders commit is to reward only the scorers as in soccer, when one person is crowned the goal king. Make no mistake, the actual scorer deserves the recognition and praise due, but a lot of players contributed to that score. If commendations aren't spread wisely, it engenders sabotage among the team members that affects the scorer. When that happens, the team loses, the organization suffers, and winning is endangered.

No matter the sport, be it a basketball or soccer game, it's a team effort. It takes someone to dribble, and it takes another to seek the right person who could connect the right pass before the scorer pounds the ball into the net.

This is the same for corporations, but not many leaders seem to know this. I am not suggesting that specific people should not be singled out for praise. After all, it takes leadership, direction, and support to get things done, so acknowledging a particular person or group is laudable. My point is that every effort should be made to also recognize and appreciate the other players who are on the team. I acknowledge nevertheless that even in sports, there are different roles and some games/season allow some players to be highlighted more than the others. That's why we have prizes for the best goalkeeper, the best defender, the best blocker, the best quarterback, most valuable player awards, and many more.

It is also good to have opposition at times. I do well with constructive opponents because they keep me on my toes. Not all opposing parties may dislike you or wish your collapse; some of them just disagree with you on principle but not as a person. It is imperative to decipher which is which and learn to work with people of that caliber. Unfortunately, when some people get to the top, they forget simple principles. Leaders in many cases do not receive genuine opinions because most of the people who surround them prefer to echo what they think the leaders want to hear in order to keep him or her happy. Because of fear of losing their job; - some sycophants will go to any length to destroy other colleagues just to gain favor. Usually, people like that don't last. A few may rise all the way to the top, but many end up disgraced. A good name is better than riches, so invest a good name. Don't assume all praise is genuine. When you are around people who are considered leaders or "higher-ups" in an organization, rather than simply praise them, speak eloquently, and to the core that adds value.

Leaders who cannot stand for what they believe in, need to re-evaluate their leadership skills. Following are some basic qualities of a good leader:

- A good leader is a visionary.
- A good leader sets the right pace.
- A good leader respects the views of others.
- A good leader preaches what he or she practices.
- A good leader seeks the advancement of his subordinates.
- A good leader seeks better ways to enhance his or her leadership.
- A good leader is willing to change direction when necessary.
- A good leader determines the best form of recognition to be given to his subordinates to stimulate them.
- A good leader, arguably, succeeds. Sometimes it may be instant, sometimes not. Some of these leaders may not be recognized as good leaders until further down the road.

- A good leader does not easily get irritated when he or she is corrected, especially when done in the right spirit.
- A good leader cannot satisfy everyone but tries to create an environment worth sacrificing for.

Caution:

A good leader may not necessarily be a good manager. People sometimes confuse these two. A manager is someone who supervises and delivers day-to-day activities and then organizes routine activities. A leader, on the other hand, is someone people look up to and who is a visionary. People may look up to managers too, but the style in which a leader communicates differs from that of a manager. Whether you are a manager or a leader, do not expect to be loved by everyone; you need to make hard decisions sometimes if you want to achieve anything. Take the right steps, but also remember that you are working with people. People are all motivated differently. Some are motivated by money; others by recognition. Some people respond to extrinsic motivation; others prefer intrinsic motivation. Find out what motivates others and provide those incentives for effective productivity.

It is troubling when a leader lacks written goals for direction. The reasons some leaders or managers do better than others is based on simple principles, including written goals, clear targets, evaluations, identifying and correcting mistakes early on, planning and forecasting, and so on. Some leaders are good at instructing but cannot follow those same instructions themselves. Some leaders act as though they have never made a mistake in life. Be wary of such leaders. A leader who admits mistakes and shares experience with guidance is usually an excellent leader. Some leaders (depending on cultural heritage) deem confrontation as negative, disrespectful, and demeaning. What some of them forget is that there is no such thing as positive confrontation, where the subordinate finds the appropriate time to discuss issues affecting their performance. As a subordinate, appreciate what you're learning but suggest ways that motivate you better to your boss in the right tone. Remember, a leader is not there to spoon-feed you. Have solutions, be articulate, and be ready to answer questions if they arise. Send a note of thanks to your boss after the meeting regardless of the outcome by appreciating his or her time and promising changes in attitude or performance as a result of the meeting.

As a leader though, just learn the skill of humility. Be firm and find the rhythm of your people, and determine which types of personalities you may need to have on your team to achieve a goal in a healthy manner.

FOOD FOR THOUGHT:

Most leaders were once subordinates, and so most of them can relate to issues relating to their expectations. It is advisable to note that times are different, so what might have been good in one era may not work anymore. The good old days may not be a great time today, so beware of that kind of mindset. Leaders should constantly read good books that enhance their leadership dexterities. A good leader should admit faults and address them immediately. Finally, a good leader should be amenable to changing direction if the current path is not going as planned.

CHAPTER 15

Guarding Against the Tongue

I have made it a point to avoid speaking when angry, disappointed, or even betrayed. At least, I try not to speak right in the heat of the moment to avoid saying something I might later regret. I still struggle sometimes in the practice of this special skill, but I try to remain silent, breathe in deeply, sleep on the issues a few days before making any comment. It only takes a few seconds to ruin the reputation you have spent years building. The tongue, is one of the smallest but most powerful body parts.

The same tongue curses and blesses, can give guidance as well as derail you, it can be boastful and it can be humble, it can talk loudly and it can also talk softly. The tongue can set a whole nation ablaze - topple governments or set it on the right course towards healing and reconciliation. Just the words that come out from your mouth can set the world on fire.

The tongue is a very small member of the body but has considerable impact when used correctly or incorrectly.

Consider the size of a ship, but it takes only a small rudder to steer it. Consider also the airplane. In spite of its size and weight, it takes only the rudder and the ailerons to control and turn the airplane from left to right. The pilot relies on the wheel to raise and lower the elevators that move it back and forward in order to be controlled.

The tongue serves as the tool that controls what comes out of our mouths—what to say, how to say it, and the level of perception we create for ourselves by what we say and how we say it. Your reputation is not just in how you present yourself but also how you control your tongue. Two different people could utter the same sentence, but their hearers may derive two sharply different meanings all because of the tone in which each must have made that statement.

Guarding against the tongue can sometimes be difficult. Sometimes you are pushed to the limit to say anything possible to get out of trouble, but that is the point where you should rather be more cautious and more in control of your tongue. Your true character reveals itself in adversity. Consider the following thoughts:

- Do you want to respond now or take a breath first?
- Will you respond in the same manner after a few days?
- Can this type of response ruin your reputation?
- Who is listening? Who is your audience?
- If God (depending on who you worship) were you, would He respond in the same manner?

After answering these questions honestly, you may be more inclined to refrain from talking in anger.

Sometimes it is best to leave the scene immediately, cool down, regain your composure, and return later if necessary. The tongue can be a powerful tool and needs to be subjugated for its better use.

Most politicians will relate to this because they may in one way or the other be faced with situations where they may be saying the right thing but at the wrong time, or just because people don't agree with their position, they lose their respect in seconds. The journalist chases after them everywhere, asking questions that sometimes aggravate them; however, if you do not restrain your composure, you may end up allowing your emotions to speak rather than your brains.

Parents, mentors, celebrities, and anyone whom someone looks up to should take note and be careful because you don't know who is admiring you from a distance.

Decent society has a pattern for how we should talk and generally live. Life should be natural of course, but there is always the right way and the wrong way. Everything has its dark side, and every coin has its opposite side. Just as Heaven has hell, so does everything have its reverse side. It's either good or bad; you cannot be lukewarm. Even God hates lukewarm people; hence His suggestion that we choose whether to be hot or cold.

There are certain people who may not be where they should be, or ought to be but for wrong choice of words. There are many people who use curse words in every sentence. This will not take them anywhere, unless, perhaps, they are stand-up comedians. They are allowed and may run away with such vulgar words, but don't imitate them foolishly.

Society is becoming more cautious about what they listen to, what influences them. It is, therefore, our duty to tilt to the tune.

The use of the tongue properly enhances one's looks and respect. Compare a physically unattractive person who carefully presents him or herself well in speech, compared to an extremely physically attractive person who is rude and disrespectful. Though the latter is physically attractive, you are most likely to gravitate to the former.

FOOD FOR THOUGHT:

Your tongue can get you into trouble if it's not under control, and that we should always watch our words and our tone to ensure we don't hurt others or ruin our reputation.

CHAPTER 16

Reaching Your Potential

"If you're always first out of the door, you'll end up last to be promoted."

- Vickie L. Milazzo, founder and owner of Vickie Milazzo Institute.

You may be the smartest person in the organization, but that doesn't constitute you needing to be the first to always leave the building and the last to come to the office. When it comes to promotion, regardless of whatever it is in life that you do, people will evaluate you and judge from all angles, fairly and unfairly. It doesn't cost to stay a few minutes longer in the office, even if you have nothing left to do, just to be among the pack to leave. You don't need to always have to wait for the pack, but when you continually abuse your opportunities, on the day that you need it most, nobody will believe you. Usually, people nickname you secretly, colleagues and your superiors might be discussing you behind your back.

I have the belief that people who stay a little longer at work and report early arguably are seen as hard workers. Consider two people: Kim and Christiana. Kim produces forty percent profit to the organization on average, stays longer, and reports to work very early most of the time; Christiana produces sixty percent profit for the same organization and has the same rank as Kim. However, Christiana always reports to work an hour later than Kim and constantly leaves work thirty minutes earlier than Kim but has excuses all the time on why she is late at work and also has to leave earlier than everyone else.

When it comes to promotion and there is only one spot available at the time, bosses might ignore the twenty percent difference between Kim and Christiana and may offer the promotion to Kim instead of Christiana because, all other factors being equal, the bosses feel they can rely more on Kim than Christiana.

Another school of thought could argue that Christiana in the previous scenario may be more respected and more likely to be promoted because she is delivering which is what they want, not more time being spent in the office costing waste, compared to Kim's. It all depends on the superior's mindset.

Reliability and trust play a pivotal role in promoting people, so you cannot just rely on your knowledge to succeed in life. In fact, I know quite a few people in life who made the highest grades in school but are almost always hungry, while others who add a little bit of 'oomph' and charisma get the cake.

Networking, knowing people, and people knowing you in return is another factor, but overall you must deliver and be trusted and reliable to get to the top.

I have seen people get promoted just because of the network they have in the institution. I have seen people getting better jobs just because of how others see them and want them. I have seen people succeed quicker in life because of whom they know. I have also seen mistakes of certain people overlooked, simply because they know someone at the top or across board. The question you should be asking yourself is, who is speaking about you in the boardroom, in the market place, at the mall, at the bar or in the washroom. Positioning oneself and networking positively is critical beyond just your technical skills, though both are needed.

FOOD FOR THOUGHT:

Working hard is good, but working smart is greater. When you do someone's job, work as though it were yours. Do for others, as you would like them to do for you. It was my elder brother who once said that anytime he worked for people, he did so with the mindset that he too would one day have his own work going and would want his workers to work hard for him. In other words, his work attitude was like a prayer. No wonder wherever he worked, he was normally singled out for praise and given even more responsibilities than he was originally employed for.

I have worked and seen some subordinates who demand more but produce little. The math doesn't work that way. If you study the lifestyles of many such people, they end up living average lives, if not below. They nag and complain about everything, and they always have a reason why something cannot be done. They always expect things to be done for them. They read only the employment laws that favor them and ignore the rest. Our role is to solve puzzles, and if we cannot, why occupy that space in the first place?

Avoid Excuses:

One of life's biggest adversaries is 'excuse' and 'procrastination'. Many people never reach their full potential because they start making excuses and give up too soon.

Human beings are the only species created that need clothing. We are meant to be creative, thoughtful, and to rule over the plants and all the rest of the creatures. But we sometimes limit ourselves against the original vision for which we were created.

One of my favorite television programs was called '*Life*', which aired on American television screens in the late 2000's and was narrated by Oprah Winfrey. In this series, different creatures were featured, from little ants on the ground to lions to deep-sea fish to many other strange creatures I had never seen nor heard of in my life until then. I saw how they managed to eat, devise strategies to survive, and constantly renew their approach to life. I saw how dolphins, in the pursuit of satisfying their hunger, outsmart the little fishes in the seas by the leader creating a circle of splashes around the fishes. These dolphins smartly wait outside the splashed waters for the fish, which got frightened by the splashed waters and jumped out—straight into the mouth of the dolphins' mouths. These dolphins created a sense of unity by doing what they do best in a synergistic manner to achieve what they want as a group.

Lions are also known for their tricks. When the lion becomes too old to hunt, it makes plans with the younger ones to grab prey. The old ones with less strength go to the other side of the road while the younger ones with their sharper teeth go to the other end. When prey approaches, the old lions roar. This frightens the prey, so it flees in the opposite direction only to land in the trap of the younger ones.

Even the lower creatures have learned that you need strategy and the wisdom to work before enjoying the fruits. In the series of that program, I saw how little animals could change themselves by transforming into a flat object, thereby making it impossible for the hungry snakes to swallow them. This is how they protect themselves and their newborn babies from such prey. I saw also for the first time a frog/toad that squeezed its body into a round ball and purposely fell off from a tall rocky hill to the bottom of the valley to escape a predator, all achieved with not even a scratch on its body. I saw animals on land, muddy grounds, and in the sea, which together shared love, fought for love even to death, and at the same time were able to recognize their enemies even when they are babies. These animals create a common sense of protection, survival, and living.

Unfortunately, human beings find it difficult to identify who their enemies are. How come we human beings cannot do better? It amazes me how we still live at the mercy and wisdom and innovation of our forefathers, who build infrastructures that we still rely on, compared to our presently creative and innovative world. Though knowledge has increased in recent times, consider what our forefathers were able to create in the past when they had little to depend on! We currently live and build on their wisdoms, for which we should always be grateful to. We sometimes give up quickly when we are under pressure, claiming we've done our best when in fact we'd just started. We need to do more, else our forefathers will be rolling in their graves in disappointment.

From "Life", I understood that every creature is there for a reason, and though some become predators or prey to each other, they also are each other's protectors. Animals that cannot run, for example, know how to hide. Animals that have short tails are hardly distraught by flies because they cannot swish them off by themselves, birds take out the ticks from their body. On the contrary, ticks, flies and other insects usually disturb animals that have long tails because they have the ammunition to fight them back.

Some animals, such as the cheetah, can run extremely fast for short distances but lack energy for long distances. Their strategy is to get as close as possible before pouncing to outrun their prey or catch up on their predators quickly.

While some other animals may not necessarily be that fast in a short run, they have constant speed and adequate energy to pursue their prey (like the rabbit) until they get their meal. I find it difficult to see animals hunt each other to bloody death, but it is educating to see how they live and survive. After all, human beings live on these animals to survive as well.

Because the tortoise is slow, its shell is hard like a stone to protect it from dangers, and it can hide within its shell against any prey. Because the elephant is slow in movement compared to the leopard and the lion, it can use its trunks to uproot trees besides being very strong and huge enough to deter predators.

If animals can devise such plans and are created for specific reasons, then you are also created for a more special reason. Studies have shown that short people live much longer and look younger than tall people. This is in no way a defense to my height, but I believe I will look good till death. Research has favored me, and I like it. Not all tall people become basketball players; there might be some other reasons why they are tall. Not every strong person plays American Football. Not every beautiful lady goes for a beauty pageant. There might be other reasons why they exist. The rationale is, everyone is created unique and special.

In terms of cultural differences, no one chooses their culture; you are born into it and should be proud of your color, origin, and who you are. Why give excuse for who you are? Why disown who you are?

There is a unique reason for sprouting out of the particular roots you stem from. Utilize the advantages therein and contribute its benefits to society. This is why, while you patronize others, who in return patronizes you. Do what you're good at and be proud of it.

I was having a chat with a European on the soil of Africa some time ago. He expressed a lamentation, which made me realize that we should cherish what we have from our varied backgrounds as our special contribution to the world and be more interested in proudly marketing what we have to others.

He said it was boring to him when he came to Africa only to be entertained with European music. Why should he buy a plane ticket and spend so much on traveling to Africa only to hear European music again? For knowledge, experience, and variety's sake at least, he wanted to hear African music in Africa.

That was all he said, but I learned a lot from it. The African has a lot to show and teach the world but may not know how invaluable that knowledge is due to an orientation that tilts his definition of quality towards what is foreign. For instance, the traditional African mostly uses herbs instead of the surgeon's scalpel to handle medical issues that call for surgery. Where you may have to use the knife with all its dangers, the traditional African only needs herbs. Broken legs have been restored just because someone tied two herbs together and placed it on the broken leg. This is great science, which the African needs to explore to augment the continent's contribution to global knowledge in medical science. Yet how can this be achieved if one does not appreciate one's roots in the first place? And till one appreciates oneself, how can one sell oneself?

Back to the animal kingdom where, metaphorically, we have to learn from animals. It is interesting that, while animals on average identify each other and form groups within their species, human generations are disoriented and full of hypocrites. Do not misunderstand me. There are numerous genuine people out there who act and do their best within the confines of their capabilities within any grouping of people, but most people bring the *"I's"* instead of *"we's"* before the team, so it sounds like, I did this and that, instead of we did this and that.

This can be observed in the corporate world, faith-based institutions, and many other organized and informal setups. There is noise about teamwork, but beneath many of these are personal agendas and the fight for personal recognition—so much in-fighting. There is nothing wrong with the *"I do"* people, but it has to be done in a manner that does not throw your neighbor under the bus. All must be appreciated. Our motives and conscience are the inner gods that play us, that advise us, that caution us, that set us on the right path. It is imperative to listen to them. Unfortunately, some don't have this conscience, or theirs may be dead. Their conscience tells them something different from what their mind tells them.

The time for excuses is over. Time for excuses should not be part of your DNA. It is time to identify your unique purpose on earth, explore it, and take your possession. This possession should in no way be about self-centeredness or greed, but for the benefit of all. When you're blessed, do not look down on other people. Do not associate yourself with only the rich or people of influence, but also be a blessing to others and the needy that look up to you. Create a balance. Sometimes, the riches come back in the form of good health, longer life, and the creation of an extended family.

My wife and I had every reason to give excuses when the tides were strong against us, when we were drowning, when it was as though we were taking two steps backward for every one step forward. But we forged ahead and supported each other as our faith was tested, and we were able to survive most storms. We shared our income with people who needed it most, from our family members to friends to people we didn't know very well, and our focus was not on their reward or thanks but to satisfy their needs. The rewards are impeccable.

Remember though that some of the people whom you may help may not even recognize you when they are at the top. Don't expect any reward from anyone you help, or else you will be disappointed. Some people are developing wrinkles simply because they have expectations from human beings who constantly disappoint them. I have a deep hole in me, and when disappointments come, I place them inside that hole and move on.

Sometimes, people who give the most excuses are ironically people who are able-bodied with no reason to give excuses. Imagine having been shot in the face, losing your nose and eyes and virtually declared physically challenged, but being able to turn things around and focus on the positive side, believing in yourself with confidence, going the extra mile for example to complete your first degree with straight A's, marrying, having a baby, and being able to cook, dress your baby, entertain your baby, and act as normal all by yourself with little help.

This is the amazing story of a young lady who experienced and survived tragedy at the age of sixteen, as shown on an episode of 20/20, April 23, 2010.

The incident did not deter her from achieving her dreams, and she turned what looked like a negative situation into a positive one. The story captivated many and inspired some people to do more. If she could do this, then this is a big encouragement for everyone to succeed in spite of all odds.

Start your story, but also allow yourself to listen to someone else's story and you will be amazed. You may be ashamed to know your story is weak. Outwardly, you may look perfect and attractive, but inwardly there is the need for a total overhaul regarding the way you think, how you limit yourself, and challenges that have engulfed you. Learn the skill of survival and surround yourself with good people you can relate to in terms of common vision and encouragement.

Moses in the Bible had one of the biggest excuses for not heeding God's call to lead. He was not eloquent; he stuttered. But he was able to lead the Israelites successfully from Egypt almost to the Promised Land.

While he initially complained about his weakness, he was provided with an answer and solution.

Even so, Moses had devised more excuses. This one was about the Israelites themselves. How would they believe that his message was from God? And so God asked what he had in his hands. The rod, he retorted. God said it was enough. He (God) was to use this rod for many of the miracles he needed to perform eventually. This rod was to turn into a snake before Pharaoh, and when the other snakes were produced, the snake from the rod swallowed them all. It was this rod that was used in parting the red seas and so on. What do you have in your hands? What is your skill? What is your expertise? What are you best at? That is your rod. Someone's rod may just be a stick to you but a special weapon for that person.

Most people struggle in life because they follow other people wrongly. Everyone is gifted with a skill, and it is up to each one of us to find our sweet spot. Instead of spending time complaining, why not spend the same time to think of the next steps? We live more in the present and not the past, so why not categorize your moves to fit today's life better? You may be looking in the wrong direction all the while, so it might be better to refocus; it is not too late.

There are some people who just are in the wrong field and holding the wrong rod. Are you one of them? Know the difference and seek counsel.

Each of my three young boys have different personalities. The first boy loves to build stuff, arranging things accurately and recreating things. He could transform anything into something else. He is very artistic and creative. He is intelligent and was the youngest in his class because he took exams and was elevated.

The second boy, on the other hand, loves academic stuff. He reads very well and is regarded as one of the top in his class, though he is one of the youngest as well. Very smart in everything academic that he does, he is nevertheless not necessarily the best in creating things. He has a very high emotional intelligence and empathy than most children his age and very articulate. You can't sway him.

The third boy loves computers and knew everything about the solar system even before he was four years old. He could correct me regarding which planet has gas chambers or rings, which one was the hottest or coldest, and why. In fact, he has combined the knowledge of his older siblings. I remember we went to a science museum, and while other kids were reading the planet system on the screen, he was able to identify it just by experimenting with the various colors. Everyone peered at him in amazement.

The point here is not to talk about my children, which I usually don't, after all, everyone's child is the best, right? But what we try to do with each of them is not to put them in one basket like kittens. We try to allow them to explore their individual talents while they go to school. We wanted them to identify their path very early in life so we could channel them to the right course. I will not be surprised, all things equal, if my first son becomes an architect or works in the creative world, while the second son without a doubt becomes a litigation attorney or a professor, and the third becomes a computer software engineer. If this changes, expect another book with updates.

I wish I had such an opportunity at their age. Their unity comes in the fact that they play together, fight together, love each other, enjoy each other's expertise, and believe each is the expert in that field. We want to avoid the excuse of if we had done it this way, it might have been this way type of story.

FOOD FOR THOUGHT:

Excuses are a form of disease. It is easy to make excuses for what you cannot do, or what seems slightly difficult. All you need is a little effort and bravery to hold on. Give yourself that extra mile to complete your journey. If everyone decided to give excuses, the human race would not have so many things that we are enjoying today. Were it so with all, who then would have gone to the moon to enable so many inventions? The Wright brothers, after a few tries, would have given up in creating the first airplane. There would have been no bridges, skyscrapers, Internet services, cell phones, etc. Don't give up. Your miracle is right around the corner; it just needs a little push to arrive. Do away with energy suckers around you; do away with excuses!

CHAPTER 17

Some Victors Over Personal Challenges

Many are the incredible people out there who have survived the odds thrown at them by life. Their bravery, determination, fortitude, perseverance, and way of seeing things differently have made a difference, which makes them worth emulating. I give great credit to their parents, guardians, adopters, supporters, loved ones, and all who played and continue to play some role in accepting them into society, and also helping in transforming their lives. They have turned from being unsung heroes to sung heroes. For the sake of example, a few of such have been identified below as a way to motivate and inspire you.

Harrison Ford, a movie icon and star in 'Air Force One', (one of my favorite movies of all time), as well as the Star Wars and Indiana Jones film series and many other films. Did you know he suffered from terrible depression in his youth, and would spend a lot of time sleeping? As you can guess, he often missed classes and had trouble keeping up with his studies. Not until he signed up for drama class was he able to overcome all of his fears and transform his life.

Can you imagine what the world would have lost if Harrison Ford never got the opportunity to sign up for that drama class? Today, he is regarded as one of the geniuses and most-loved Hollywood actors of all time.

If our life's success is only determined by the grades we make in school, Harrison might have been relying on Social Security for a living today. Alas, life is far beyond that. He needed to find what would work for him, and when he did, he was able to let his talents shine.

Abraham Lincoln, the sixteenth President of the United States, serving from March 4, 1861, until his assassination in April 1865. Lincoln closely supervised the victorious Union war effort, especially the selection of top generals, including Ulysses S. Grant. There have been reports that Abraham Lincoln may have suffered from what they then called melancholia, basically today's form of depression. Most of his life prior was filled with sorrow, tragedies, misfortunes, and deaths. He was one of the only presidents who lost a son while serving in the White House. He grew up poor and in hardship, and he failed in so many ventures; however, through persistence, determination, and personal courage, and with support from a few, he rose to become one of the prominent American presidents who ever lived. He had an interesting leadership mindset. He was a Republican and initially supported slave trade; however, after a series of events, he was humbled enough to have a change of heart and support emancipation. Abraham Lincoln has left one of the most indelible legacies for American history through his personal life, leadership, and political stand. He is especially inspiring given all the challenges and trials he suffered throughout his life. He stood tall above all odds.

Brooke Shields, had the money and everything fame could bring along, including a pleasant marriage. The birth of her child, however, caused her to suffer severe postpartum depression. The situation worsened so fast that it soon had reached the point where the mere sight of a window was enough suggestion that she jumped out of it to end her misery. She was suddenly conscious of feeling inadequate, hence ashamed of herself as she battled with the emptiness within her. She could be so depressed that she sometimes ignored the baby's cry.

Fortunately, she was able to recover from her post-partum depression and had a good time as a mother. This was also mainly for various supports and compassion she received, amongst many other things. People who didn't know her well might have never known she had any problems. She may have been driving the best cars and flying first-class all over the world, flashing smiles outwardly to reporters and onlookers, but within, Brook was dealing with more than anyone would have imagined.

Diana, Princess of Wales, popularly known as "Lady Di," needs no introduction. Lady Di was the first wife of Charles, Prince of Wales. In the late 1980s, their marriage publicly began showing cracks and eventually fell apart. It was an event at first suppressed and then sensationalized.

Lady Di, with all the luxuries that she enjoyed, was incredibly unhappy while married to the Prince, and she battled depression and an eating disorder throughout her adult life. She had to create her own path of happiness through charity work, traveling all over the world. She had to learn how to conduct public speaking, was in need of love, was depressed and frustrated; however, she found joy in her two sons, William and Harry, through it all.

She tried as much as possible to care for her children herself, in terms of feeding, waking up with them, taking them to the field to play, etc. She had been a kindergarten teacher prior to dating the Prince, so it was easy for her to do.

I can recall just like yesterday that early Sunday morning in September 1997. While preparing for church, I heard over the local news about her demise in France. I wept and my mood was somber throughout the week. Some of us had looked up to her from a distance and admired her work. Yes, of course, we may not know the details and everything behind the scenes, but from what the cameras showed, she was doing great as she captivated the entire world with her charm, beauty, honesty, charity, and simplicity. I saw her hugging and holding children with AIDS wearing no gloves. She might have left the world physically, but she still lives in the hearts, minds, and souls of many people due to her passion, eloquence, and the unique impact she had made in the lives of many people, regardless of sex, color, religion, or beliefs.

John Fitzgerald Kennedy, simply known as JFK, was the thirty-fifth president of the United States, serving from 1961 until his assassination in November 1963 in Dallas, Texas. Although he suffered from various illnesses, including asthma, Kennedy always appeared strong and rugged in public and enjoyed working out and playing sports with his family. Even during his campaign, he was suffering a lot during those grueling trips across various states, but little did the spectators know about this. He sometimes had to be on medication, or on a sick bed while on those trips, but stood firm and strong when he had to go out to speak.

JFK won the election as well as the hearts of many minorities because he appeared and appealed to the average working person. At that time, Martin Luther King Jr. was traveling the cities across the US States and campaigning for freedom for people of color and the minority. Race was a big issue in the 1960s, and segregation of blacks was still common. Blacks were not allowed to board certain buses or visit certain places. At one point, King himself was in a Georgia jail. He had been arrested as part of a peaceful group attempting to integrate an Atlanta department store dining room. While the rest of the protesters had been released, King was still imprisoned on unrelated traffic charges. In those days, black voters often voted Republican and were voting specifically for Richard Nixon. However, when King was still in jail, Nixon, who allegedly had close ties with Martin Luther King Jr., did not take the stance to release him or show public sympathy. Immediately, internal discussion took place in the Kennedy camp to take advantage of the situation in their favor.

According to documentaries and research, Kennedy did take that advantage by simply expressing sympathy to Coretta Scott King over her husband's plight. Many of his aides opposed the call because it likely meant they would lose votes in the South. But Kennedy played a major role in King's release. King was released from jail shortly afterward, and reports of Kennedy's concern energized the African American community to vote for Kennedy instead of Nixon. Many historians believe that was the pivotal moment that shifted crucial votes in Northern states away from Richard Nixon to give JFK his razor-thin victory. King, immediately after his release, made a statement that he understood Candidate Kennedy had played a major role in his release, and he thereby sent an indirect message to black voters to vote for Kennedy. Interestingly, ever since, the majority of African Americans vote Democrat till date.

Kennedy found a niche where he fit, waited for the right moment, and then took action. It worked for him at the time. This is in no way to suggest that Kenney was an opportunist to win votes and not genuinely wanting to help MLK. He was genuine about his intentions, however, strategic at the same time.

The bottom line is, Kennedy could have used his sickness to easily give up on the campaign, but he persisted to his victory and changed the family name forever after his father Joe.

SOME VICTORS OVER PERSONAL CHALLENGES

Stevie Wonder is an American singer-songwriter, multi-instrumentalist, and record producer. Blind from infancy, Wonder signed with Motown Records at age twelve, and he continues to perform and record for the label to this day. It is thought that he received excessive oxygen in his incubator when he was born, which led to retinopathy, a destructive ocular disorder affecting the retina, characterized by abnormal growth of blood vessels, scarring, and sometimes retinal detachment.

Despite this ailment, Stevie lives a happy-looking life. He has achieved more success than millions of seeing people combined. He had every excuse for an obvious failure, but he moved beyond that to produce some of the best songs the world has enjoyed and continues to enjoy.

In an interview with former President Jerry John Rawlings of Ghana, he narrated how he and Stevie flew together in Europe. Since Rawlings himself was a pilot by profession, he was able to fly, and so he allowed Stevie to fly the plane by coaching him at some point during their flight experience. According to the former president, he wanted to inform the media about it at the time, but Mr. Wonder advised otherwise.

Stevie Wonder is a delight to know and is loved by many. Most importantly, he is a human example to emulate as far as his professional achievements are concerned.

Helen Keller is an American author, activist, and a lecturer who was the first deaf and blind person to graduate from college. She was not originally born blind and deaf; when she was only nineteen months old, she came down with an illness that left her deaf and blind. It was thought that the illness might have been wrongly diagnosed as *"an acute congestion of the stomach and the brain"* which could possibly have been scarlet fever or meningitis. Though the illness left her deaf and blind, it did not stop her from pursuing her dream to become a world-famous speaker and author. She is remembered as an advocate for people with disabilities, women's suffrage, and more.

Sometimes people who suffer tragedy do better than people who don't. Could it be because they have something to fight for? Could it also be it is because those who do not suffer any tragedy take things for granted? Whatever it is, it informs you about how far the human potential could take you if fully tapped. Helen used hers well in the public and private fields. She is no doubt an inspiration and lived a life worthy of emulation as far as her determination, courage, impact, and success are concerned.

Now let's take a closer look at this hero, **Harriet Tubman**, who was a slave throughout her youth, treated like an animal until she eventually escaped captivity. When she finally reached Canada, she did not stay to enjoy her freedom. She instead returned to the South and brought hundreds of black slaves to safety and freedom via the underground railroad. After a severe wound to the head, which was inflicted by a slave owner before her escape, she suffered vision impairment and seizures, but that did not keep her from fighting for the freedom of her people.

Tubman made a mark in her lifetime. Her unselfish desire to help others escape the horrors of slavery and her willingness to put herself in danger to save others was heroic.

We need more of the Harriet Tubman's to stand tall in society. You probably have not had to go through what Harriet went through, but you can still be a voice for others, an advocate for the desperate, and a blessing to those who need it.

I happen to have many friends from different cultures who are advocates, and they are gradually changing the course of my actions in life. I enjoy seeing many such friends who gather in volunteering activities in diverse communities and organizations just to support any human life that is oppressed. These are the Tubman's in disguise. They create a sense of *"we are all one people,"* and the color of their skin does not deter them from doing what is right and bringing change.

Tragedies can be blessings in disguise. They are not pleasant experiences, but they can bring positive changes and outcomes.

Louis Braille became blind after he accidentally stabbed himself in the eye with his father's awl. He later became an inventor and designed the Braille reading and writing system. This enables people who are blind or impaired vision to read and write. The Braille system works by using raised dots to represent the letters of the print alphabets. This concept was beneficial to all blind people from around the world and is still today. Had it not been for Louis Braille's blindness, he may not have invented this useful system for others experiencing similar condition to benefit from it.

SOME VICTORS OVER PERSONAL CHALLENGES

Tragedies often occur for a reason, although that reason may not be readily apparent. Instead of spending the rest of your life nagging, complaining, mulling, gossiping, and disbelieving, why not spend ninety percent of that time looking forward?

In some parts of the world, once you suffer a form of disability, you are regarded as useless and deemed a pariah, incapable of contributing to society. You almost never see a disabled person elevated as minister of state or leading any major corporation. It is as though being a disabled person automatically quarantines you from the world, and probably suggests you don't have any worthy contribution to society. This must stop. Let's give everyone an equal chance to exhibit and achieve the full potential in them regardless of disability, ability, age, sexual orientation or gender, religion, or beliefs. There is something special in all of us, and we should all have the opportunity to find that something special and use it for the greater good.

If Louis Braille had not been given the air to see himself as normal, and he as well did not allow his circumstances to cripple him, there would probably not have been an invention called braille reading, thereby limiting others who need it most. God knows best what He is doing. Let's give everyone the chance to develop.

Denzel Washington, one of the best movie actors of all time, who has arguably bridged the gap between black and whites, crossed different races and is mostly loved by his uniqueness and eloquence, focus and determination. He has won the hearts of many. No wonder he is on record as the first black to receive Emmys in the 90s.

He was born into a Christian home with his father being a priest and mother, hair stylist. Unfortunately, at age fourteen, his parents divorced, which affected their home into now, a house. His mother took over Denzel and told him she didn't know how to do it but they would figure it out.

Denzel, sensing trouble regarding the type of unpleasant life that was immediately available and easy to join, though tempted at an early stage to try a street lifestyle, that obviously wouldn't offer him anything better in return, he started attending the Boys Club in his neighborhood, which helped shape his character. He took also to helping his mother at her beauty parlor, listening to those who came around and discussed their stories from love life, relationships, and issues at home. He listened to all that while pretending he wasn't. These stories immensely helped and shaped him to become a better storyteller. No wonder he is best known and at his best when he leads movies that entail an exchange of words aside defending others and his community.

At the time (in the '60s), it was believed that, the widow of Malcolm X who was a friend to Denzel's mother, usually came to the salon. It was said she played a pivotal role in Denzel's life because it was revealed that, a lady prophesied into his life for greatness, which was believed to be Malcolm X's wife. At this time, he was nothing, however, this lady saw something unique in Denzel. According to research, the lady continued to say, he would be traveling the entire world and be very famous. He would be successful and many people would listen to him and he would be the eye for many.

Assuming it was not even the widow of Malcolm X who said all those things, whoever it was, Denzel took it, believed it and worked at it, and the reality is another story to be written. He is admirable, giving, a promoter, and a wealthy family man. He has indeed traveled the globe, he is famous, he has great vision and has achieved even more than he was told he would be. He did not just sit down and enjoy the prophecy, he worked at it, unlike most believers today. They will pray without ceasing but refuse to work at what their destiny is designed for, unfortunately, may leave this earth with their 'music never sang'. Was God a liar? No. There is an action element to any prophecy, and Denzel did just that.

In his own words, during an interview in 2017, he admitted welcoming the great Nelson Mandela in his house secretly for a number of days. This was never known to the public, at least not to a lot of people until he announced it, and this was a few years after Mandela passed on. He jokingly talked about how Mandela enjoyed fried chicken aside the basic and simple food, which was specially prepared by Denzel's wife, and how they enjoyed their unions until this icon returned to South Africa.

I don't think Nelson Mandela would just visit anyone if he didn't have the respect and a sense of protection from such a person. Denzel offered these. They might have shared similar sentiments and goals, they might have mutually admired each other at different levels but staying together in one house was another admirable thing to hear. Denzel has achieved more than he expected and far more than the prophecy.

In all these, the most intriguing part of Denzel's story is how he turned a very negative situation into a successful one. Now, he is seen as one of the most positive, inspiring personalities and one who walks the talk.

FOOD FOR THOUGHT:

Excuses are necessary tools for incompetence and failure. If all these people above, could withstand their challenges to sail on top of their careers and life, how much more those who have everything going for them physically? There should be no space for excuses for anyone not achieving their dream. All spring from the mindset one has. Every good and evil, first comes from one's thoughts, and as to how to process these thoughts depends on the individual. So, it depends on which one chooses to entertain, considering the future, the pros and cons.

It is my belief that, we have all been given unique abilities to perform our duties on earth and to perform them well. We tend to envy others when we are incapable of achieving anything. Why envy someone who is running in his own track? Maybe that's not your calling; yours may be something you have not yet identified. Maybe also, you are being motivated to identify your goal, pursue it with diligence, and do better.

I learned in my early life that in order to conquer your fears, it takes commitment and focus, and you must believe in yourself first. We sometimes undermine our abilities, as a result, we achieve very little. We settle in our comfort zone and refuse to grow. Growth is part of life, and though we grow by default in age and stature, our minds sometimes don't grow at the same pace. If you have a problem with speech, learn how to speak and attend communication seminars. If your issue is shyness, take courses that could help you come out of your shell. Whatever it is, there is an antidote that is available. Look for the solution rather than focusing on the difficulties.

All of these will depend on you as well. It is one thing desiring to grow or improve and another thing to actually do it.

✶   ✶   ✶

CHAPTER 18

A Sense of Commonality

It is important to decipher between commonality and having common ground. While commonality seeks to address, not only areas where one or two people naturally possess something similar on which they can dwell to build a relationship, it also addresses areas where one can learn a skill to create a sense of commonality. Common ground, on the other hand, seeks to focus on compromise, mostly for the sake of peaceful negotiation to resolve a pending issue.

The goal, however, is not to determine if common ground or commonality is the best. This chapter is written to support the premise of the power of commonality and what it can bring, not just economically, but also socially, psychologically, mentally, and sensibly. This chapter focuses on a common-sense approach to achieving what one desires by understanding the power of commonality. Numerous examples and practical lessons have been provided to help you understand how commonality works to take advantage - no matter the environment.

I had a professor who was an ex-military personnel called Todd, whom I learned a lot from by simply observing him. He once said, *"beauty only lasts for just five minutes when you join a new firm. After that grace period, you will need to perform to be recognized"*. For you to have that commonality with your team, you must deliver. Your beauty again shows only after you are performing and maintaining a respectable pace. This has proven to be very true. I remember joining a reputable Fortune 500 company immediately post my Master's degree. On the very first day, after just a few pleasantries, it was like déjà vu. I was met with dozens of spreadsheets with headwind numbers to study, analyze, and report on. The smile I had on my face vanished for a while, but I regained it after I gained control over myself because I immediately recalled what that professor said. I was smiling to myself when it happened to me exactly the way it was narrated. My commonality in the group would only be sustained when I delivered on what I was expected to analyze for our group. Commonality also in terms of adding value and having a sense of belonging.

"Uncommon success is found on the spiritual plane; you can't get there through common convention or following others. Hard work is not enough; many work slavishly hard for little reward. Intelligence is insufficient; how many educated and brilliant people there are who fail utterly and completely. Goodness is not enough; how many meek and good souls do demigods to fertilize their golden crops till into the earth like manure. There is something more—it is the unseen essential, and everyone has access to it".

- Bryant McGill

WHY THE NEED FOR COMMONALITY?

Commonality is needed in all forms and shapes. It's all around us. Commonality helps us to be better people, especially in areas where you may naturally have things in similar with someone, for example, by the food you eat and the neighborhood you come from. However, you may need to learn how to play Golf for example, to complete that aspect of commonality with that person. If you want to connect with learned people, it will be wise to read and educate yourself to be at their level of understanding. It is important because it helps connect like-minded people together. Simple as that!!! It is only in having things in common that there exists peace in certain parts of the world. It is also the reason that some neighbors are able to coexist. Commonality allows you the power to connect with people easily due to the confidence that comes with it. Also, it helps you identify attributes in general that are healthy for you to potentially connect with someone easily.

I was at the playground with my three sons one time when I met this lady who narrated how a neighbor of hers wouldn't speak to anyone, say hello to anybody, or have eye contact. The entire street where they lived seemed odd, as no one actually practiced hospitality. Not so long ago, they saw ambulances blinking in front of this guy's house. He'd had a heart attack or something similar. Neighbors could be your first aid in times of emergency. Be nice to your neighbors, folks. You don't need scientific evidence to understand this. I know the world has become so dangerous that trust has also become an expensive commodity, but we should attempt to give it a try once again, though cautiously.

SETTING UP A SCENARIO ON LOW AND HIGH COMMONALITY:

Let's consider the following scenarios;

A group of different career personnel, from different cultures, all dressed in their supposed attires,

1. Business professional attire – who are Indians
2. People wearing ordinary clothes – who are all Caucasians or whites
3. Another group also wearing ordinary clothes – only this time is a combination of different races
4. A group wearing medical uniform – who form a combination of different races but are mostly doctors

In this same room enters a black person, let's call him Fredua, dressed ordinarily. Which group do you think he or she would join?

Hypothetically, it is believed Fredua would join the group with the mixed race because that person has a much stronger commonality there than the group dressed ordinarily but all Caucasians. Will Fredua feel intimidated by the medical professionals because of their profession and how they are dressed? Will Fredua disregard the Indian group because of their outfit in the first place?

To test this hypothesis, I conducted my own experiment with different scenarios, which I will discuss in the chapter that follows. The scenarios were not exactly the same as the one above, but they were close enough to draw a legitimate conclusion.

SYNERGY AND COMMONALITY

I asked Steve, an eighty-three-year-old friend, during one of our usual lunch together, what he would do when confronted with the above circumstance. His answer was straight and simple; 'no matter what the group may be', he asserted that, he would look out for the most beautiful ladies to sit with, regardless of color, career, and race or how they were dressed. We burst into a bout of helplessly long laughter simultaneously.

As a matter of fact, the solution to the above narration will depend on many factors and differ from person to person and group to group.

I met Steve, who has become a very good friend of mine, at a function. We bonded immediately on a single note. Initially, it was another eighty-two-year-old lady who opened a door for Steve. I had immediately rushed to help, but she had insisted and kept the door open for me instead. I felt a bit of shame as I went through, as my natural self would have loved to open the door for her. She, however, beat me to it. All the same, she immediately invited me to sit with them outside the hotel near the swimming pool for lunch. This group included a younger doctor friend of theirs. The four of us began to chat about life, and also about the businesses that had brought us there. We also talked about our backgrounds, spouses, and daytime businesses. We really gelled like people who had known each other for a long time.

After a pleasant lunch, we exchanged business cards and pleasantries. A special bond between us had been built, especially with Steve, the gentleman. After that day, we continued to meet up for lunches and home visits, sometimes with the entire family coming along. My boys were younger at the time, the oldest only six years old, so you can imagine I was nervous about their behavior. The three boys spent time chasing each other in Steve's residence, despite the pleas from my wife and me—*"Stop it! Don't do that! We are in someone else's house!"* It was as though I was flaming the fire for them to do more. They would listen and pretend to be polite for a while, but once we turned aside for a minute, they would start up again.

Yet my wonderful friends were rather enjoying the kids while we the parents were so distressed. They couldn't stop commenting on how cute, awesome, sweet, and polite they felt the boys were. Really???...

During one particular lunch with Steve at his favorite Indian restaurant, he said this to me (paraphrased): *"Evans, I wouldn't be here if we didn't share a common bond. I like your sense of intelligence, humor, energy, and the fact that we share ideas together."*

I was in the process of writing this book when he said that. In fact, I had written quite a few lines that morning before meeting him, so it was like he was being used to provide additional practical lines to the book, and as a matter of fact, affirming my conviction to write this book in the first place.

I was quiet for some time after he had spoken, and then I told him about the book I was writing and how exactly he was on the topic. I listened to him, shared his wisdom, and thought about what he was educating me on with regard to ancient history. I requested to be one of his students (despite his age, he still lectures in one of the major institutions in the nation), and I also love history and especially desired to know more about him.

FOOD FOR THOUGHT:

The above incident was possible and took place only because of the same values and commonality that we shared, regardless of age, experience, race, color, ethnicity, and or sexual orientation.

Commonality opens doors for you, and so needs to be used wisely. Your credibility and the integrity you possess will become the tool that sustains the relationship in the long run.

CHAPTER 19

Research on Case Studies Regarding Commonality

In the process of writing this book, I conducted practical research among different types of personalities to try to determine their way of thinking in relation to different topics discussed below. The following summarizes the different groups of people I conducted the interview on:

Group A: This group included senior business executives between the ages of thirty to sixty years and beyond. These were mostly married people with children and were black, selected purposely for this study.

Group B: Group B was made up of working-class of whites, both male and female, most of who had children, and were also purposely selected for the sake of the study.

Group C: The third group, C, consisted of selected individuals who were a mix of young millennials, and a motley collection of people from diverse background in terms of education, careers, experiences, and who formed a natural blend of the world as far as origin, color of skin, culture, and ethical norms were concerned (whites, blacks, indians, hispanics etc.). As well, they were students and in the working class purposely chosen for the research.

Following are the four case studies I presented to them, some in a specific time frame to complete it, and some during a major executive lecture session, having had the opportunity as part of my business strategy consulting life while on lecturing duty.

It is to be noted that the answers portray a true reflection of what they think but may not necessarily be true in your case. Finally, these people were not pushed to answer in a particular way, nor were they influenced by any circumstances or prompted through any leading mannerism to provide certain answers. They freely and willingly answered as best as they could.

Results gathered from the groups were an interesting exercise, I must say. Except for a few groups that were put together specifically for this purpose, most of the rest of the participants provided their answers discreetly and independently. Find below both the compiled survey and its related results summarized based on affinity.

CASE 1:

A white medical doctor enters a room where there are other medical doctors, but they are all black. In the same room are other white-skinned professionals, including lawyers, architects, and bankers who are gathered at a common place.

In another part of the room is a group of mixed professionals, students, whites, Asians, and black people, which had also gathered and are engaged in conversation.

Which group would the white medical doctor join? Discuss!

CASE 1'S RESULTS:

As an eye opener, because there was conversation going on in the room, it indicates that nothing formal had started yet, in terms of official sitting and formal program. Still, this does not indicate that the results would have been any different.

In their view, depending on how educated he is on issues of race, what his stance is on social and/or racial justice issues, his own social location, upbringing, whether he was raised in a mixed-race situation, he might approach the group of doctors or mixed group. If he is not aware of these things, he might approach the white group, says one millennial in Group C.

Another member of the millennial group stated it would depend if he knew members of the other groups, as that would determine where to gravitate towards. If the doctor doesn't know anyone in any other group other than the medical professionals, then he would be naturally inclined to the medical group.

Only a few respondents believed the white doctor would join other professionals who looked like him for familiarity.

However, the overwhelming majority from all the three groups believed regardless of race or culture, the white medical doctor would most naturally gravitate to the medical professionals (who were people of color).

According to some, common professional experience and interest carries more weight than any racial issues, so the commonality is related more to the profession than to skin color.

A few others cemented that decision by stating that common interest and peer attraction would be some of the reasons he would join those who share his profession.

According to a section in Group C, medicine is less about the color of the skin and more about the knowledge that people can extract and share with one another. The variable in this would be what type of event it is. If it were a social event, then maybe he would gravitate toward the other white people, but if this were a professional event where the doctor hopes to meet with other professionals, then the doctor would no doubt choose to be in the spot with the other doctors, especially if they are wearing their uniforms.

* * *

CASE 2:

A black military personnel who is dressed head to toe in his military uniform is invited into a conference, in a room that is fully packed with different people by the time he arrives. Upon entering the room to take his seat, he realizes there is no usher available to direct him to a particular seat. He sees there are four empty chairs sprinkled throughout the room. One chair is in front of a group of people who are the same race as he is, but who are non-military. They are casually dressed in hooded sweatshirts and jeans. Another chair is next to a group comprised of individuals who are white and wearing military uniforms like him. The third chair is in front of a group made up of hispanics in medical uniform, and the fourth chair was with a group made up of professors, ordinary people, and invited guests like him.

Please note that, this group's composition comprises of different races including men and women.

Which chair (or group) do you think this military gentleman would decide on and why? Discuss!

CASE 2'S RESULTS:

As a side note, the description of this case indicates, unlike the first one, an official program had begun by the time this uniformed gentleman arrived.

One respected professor in Group B who lectures at a major university in the US indicated he would guess the military person would sit with his brothers in arms. The military, he explained, is the most fully integrated, least racist organization in the world, by far. Therefore, he would sit with his fellow service members.

This was reinforced by the rest of the Groups (A and C). In particular, someone in Group C stated that the military builds a strong sense of camaraderie among members.

Another person in Group A also made the case that the military, and, for that matter, the uniform in itself is representing the armed forces, so a military person cannot afford to join just any group.

Though there were one or two additions from the groups in terms of how it may depend on other factors, considering the overwhelming answer and result from each member of the three groups, I should conclude that, about ninety nine percent agreed on the fact that the military always stays military regardless of skin color. Therefore, in this case, the decision on commonality has more to do with the profession than any other consideration.

✶ ✶ ✶

CASE 3:

A young student was invited to a major event. Upon arriving, he was met by other older professionals who were dressed as classily as he was. The only difference was these professionals were much older and more accomplished than he was.

In the same room were a group of other students who were more shabbily dressed (baggy jeans, untucked shirt, etc.).

The third group consisted of diverse types of people in terms of their skin color, culture, age, diverse professions and the way they dressed.

Which group would this student prefer to join? Discuss!

CASE 3'S RESULTS:

In this scenario, nothing suggested that the program had already begun, as it was vague. However, reading between the lines indicates the program may not have officially begun. Also, it was not clear if the gathering was a job event, professional setting, or social.

A member from Group B assessed it as this; the first and second groups offered no option as far as the situation was concerned. Students, according to the member, are most comfortable with people they are used to. He cited a typical example on campus and affirmed the third group would be a much greater possibility. A marketing executive pal in the UK in the same group affirms the previous person's view in an independent format, saying, expecting the student was young, though not stated, the student would naturally avoid the older group. And as the younger group wasn't dressed like him, hence potentially may not have similar interests or tastes, the student would join the diverse group.

The only aspect missing from the description of the diverse groups was whether they were diverse also in age, gender, and/or sexual orientation. In this case, it is assumed the focus is on ethnicity, but as we've used the term "diverse," the student was more likely to find a number of people within that group with enough commonality to chat with.

However, there was an interesting assessment from someone in Group C. He determined that it would depend on the intentions and goal of the student and what image one wanted to portray. If the student was there to network and meet professionals, there is the likelihood that the student might join the mixed and/or professional group. Otherwise stated, the student might join the shabbily dressed peer group. The participant continued to posit that he believed the well-dressed student might end up mingling with all the groups, basically due to what he wanted, knowing the passion of students.

The earlier result from Group B was aligned with some of the results derived from Group A; however, most of them immediately added that if these professionals are in his dream profession, this student would likely join the well-dressed professionals to network.

This was affirmed by a successful business guru friend of mine in Group B (President of a major franchise company) without knowing what others might have infused. He said that if the student was attending the program for entertainment only, he would more than likely join the third group of diverse people. If he were, however, attending the major event for networking or professional purposes, he would join the group of older professionals.

Contrary to some assertions, some of the members in Group C insisted that the student would prefer to join the group of older professionals who were dressed classily because their energy would be fresh, welcoming, and uplifting. However, another subgroup and some individuals believed that it would depend on the motivation for the student being at this event. If the older professionals were in the position to help the student's career prospects in any way, the student would stay with the older group and network. In that sense, they see the student staying with the older professionals for most of the night and then migrating to the spot that had the diverse group of people to close out the night. Others also agreed, adding that they see this student mingling with the older professionals for reasons of friendship or mentorship.

✶ ✶ ✶

CASE 4:

A professor was invited to a major country's Presidential Palace, or what is referred to in American as 'White House' or in the United Kingdom as 'No 10'. The invitation was to honor him with other colleagues, but the rule was that she be allowed to sit wherever she wanted and would be called up when it was time. She arrived quite early and found a comfortable seat in a corner.

Within a few minutes, the rest of the guests started arriving. A large group of people decided to sit near this professor; however, it was made up of ordinary people from the society who had only been invited to be part of the ceremony. It was a networking session at the time, so all was just milling around and connecting with each other.

She then realized there were other professors gathered in a nice corner engaged in conversation, laughing, and sharing their success stories. These professors, however, were younger and had lower accreditations than she was.

Then a final group of respected dignitaries from all backgrounds came in and found a common spot where they all decided to sit. Each of these groups had enough space to accommodate this professor in case she decided to change seat.

What do you think this accomplished professor would do and why? Discuss!

CASE 4'S RESULTS:

In this scenario, it was clearly stated that the initial time was spent on networking, and the formal program hadn't started yet.

A subset of interviewees in Group A concluded that the professor initially may desire to interact with the ordinary people as a way of courtesy, and to leave an impact with this new set of people. Afterwards, she would eventually gravitate towards the professionals who naturally fell in her network.

This was affirmed by another subset in the same group, which expressed the belief that she would remain where she sat at first. She would prefer to wait to be called and invited to sit at another place after everybody had settled in.

A different subgroup of participants in Group B also affirmed the above assertion by stating that the professor would stay and talk with the ordinary people around where she was seated, unless she was uncomfortable. They went on to state that she may then move to the other two groups or find one of the three that she was most comfortable with. She would definitely talk to people from all the three groups, since she had greater commonality with the group of professors than with the other group of dignitaries.

In this same scenario, half of the survey interviewees in Group C agreed with the assertions of groups B and A, while the other half believed the professor would gravitate towards the younger professors to serve as an icon and mentor, get to know what they were up to, and the like.

Another school of thought arising from most of the other members in other groups also felt it would depend on her expectation. If she knew anyone in other groups, including that of her profession, it would be the only reason she may consider changing position.

* * *

GENERAL REFLECTIONS REGARDING THE CASES AND BEYOND:

It was fascinating analyzing all the results and reading different views from different brains with diverse backgrounds in terms of their socio-cultural environment, how they were raised, their current status, age, culture, gender, experience, and so on. The above results only go to affirm the beauty of our diversity and how we all see things. There are neither right nor wrong answers, nor is there anything wrong with any of the results derived above. It is purely based on a combination of various factors, including reality and perception.

My sister, Michella, who was studying to become an attorney of Law at the time (she is now), flew to the US from her home base, UK to write the New York bar exams a while ago. While she was doing some research in one of the libraries near where I lived, someone approached her and asked if she was also writing the New York bar exams. This person had also flown down from one of the Arab countries for the same purpose. What attracted the gentleman to speak with my sister was the pile of law books that was in front of her. Under normal circumstances, this gentleman had nothing in common with my sister because they did not speak the same language and did not appear to be from the same culture or continent. However, he found this commonality with my sister, based on the books she was studying. The type of books you read could connect you to someone who shares similar interests.

RESEARCH ON CASE STUDIES REGARDING COMMONALITY

Outside the study above, it is generally believed that military personnel, for example, usually pay allegiance to each other regardless of color, gender, origin, race, or nationality. Therefore, another scenario in a form of hypothesis was created saying, If you have a big room filled with different classes of people including doctors, nurses, politicians, military personnel, students, and kids to mention few, and you group them based on their field of expertise or commonality, and on the other hand you intentionally create equal space amongst each common group and bring in individuals who also belong to at least one of these groups, you will find out that these individuals would sit or join the group that they have the same commonality with.

People who work in the same profession usually relate much more quickly than those who are in different professions. A police officer in the US would usually relate to another police officer in Kenya for example. Politicians in Uganda may quickly relate to one another in another country whether in the United Arab Emirates or Egypt or Australia, because they speak the same language as far as their professions are concerned. This applies to every profession regardless of geographic location.

The bottom line is we use commonality to do business, relate to each other, have fun, share common dreams, enjoy one another's company, and so on. There are many successful stories of people who use the right channel to reach the king's heart. There are also many stories of unsuccessful people who use the wrong channel (unknown to them) and never got what they wanted. Knowledge and wisdom exist, but it is known that the application of wisdom is better than just acquiring it.

It is because of such commonalities that companies interview potential candidates to determine which is fit. As a candidate, your duty is to research and determine the 'right language' to speak in order to relate to individuals in that organization. This is the art of commonality in disguise. It is an interesting terrain, which cannot be avoided. If you wish to avoid it, then you are better off on your own creating your path of success and then resetting the rules to follow.

SYNERGY AND COMMONALITY

"...Commonality with other people carries with it all the meanings of the word common. It means belonging to a society, having a public role, being part of that which is universal. It means having a feeling of familiarity, of being known, of communion. It means taking part in the customary, the commonplace, the ordinary, and the everyday. It also carries with it a feeling of smallness, or insignificance, a sense that one's own troubles are "as a drop of rain in the sea." The survivor who has achieved commonality with others can rest from her labors. Her recovery is accomplished; all that remains before her is her life".

- Judith Lewis Herman, Trauma and Recovery:
"The Aftermath of Violence - From Domestic Abuse to Political Terror"

At a point in the height of my career, I was privileged to have been 'headhunted' to lead a major institution outside the US. Even though it was my native country and I was familiar with the general terrain, to a large extent, I hadn't been there permanently for many years. Hence, to some extent, I had lost touch with the cultural systems and how they went about doing things. Over the short period I was there, I had to relearn everything and teach new things at the same time. These new teachings may not be popular but it was the best practices for which I was invited.

Before I made the difficult decision to accept the offer and go, a friend who was in the UK had introduced me to another friend of his who had also just relocated to that same country and who, coincidentally, had also been headhunted by a major Gold Mining Company. I emailed this new friend, and when I arrived, we connected, had lunch, and later had many more such lunches and dinners and even traveled together a lot. Soon, we became so close that we transitioned from friendship to brotherhood. We shared common careers and similar goals, so it was comfortable and mutually beneficial professionally to always be together. In fact, we shared family systems and beliefs together, and at the time I had lost both parents, I became close to his parents. His siblings became my siblings, especially one of his most senior sisters. Why? Simple! The power of commonality.

RESEARCH ON CASE STUDIES REGARDING COMMONALITY

Our closeness was as a result of the many commonalities we shared and believed in. I am sure the friend who introduced us would be surprised to see how far we'd taken our friendship, and I am not sure they share a similar bond like we do. Career, goals, aspirations, sense of humor, common places of interest, and so on bring people together. How you use these and take positive advantage of them depends entirely on the individual. Though I was and still am close to the friend who introduced me to this new friend, the difference is that my other friend and I had known each other for over thirty years of our lives, we played table tennis together at a tender age when at the time we were just slightly taller than the table tennis board. We shared each other's homes, visited each other during vacations while young, and stayed with each other during our early careers. We loved each other because without a doubt we shared almost everything in common.

However, at a point in time (no one's fault), our relationship drifted a bit. It's not that we didn't like each other anymore, but our paths in terms of career in particular, had taken a different lane. He was extremely academically focused and in the finance world. He lived with me with my mother (now deceased) and other siblings in his earlier career life just after graduating from his first degree, so he would come home from work and run to watch business news. This didn't amuse me. I was, on the other hand, kind of stalled a bit in terms of academic progress and was heavily interested in fun stuff than academic issues. I loved sports highlights, soap-operas, and various television series. This infuriated him, and I believe he deemed me not serious (though he couldn't tell me to my face) compared to him. Working in a financial institution, he felt he understood life better in many ways that I did not and which didn't make sense to me at the time.

Make no mistake, I had goals, vision, and knew what I was doing too, but how I directed my aspirations was totally different from him. This obviously could not enable us to share similar goals any longer, however, we continue to remain friends, just on separate paths on career.

Unlike my other friend, who was and is a kind-hearted person, my new friend and I share in common, almost everything you can think of. In particular, we share a career path, so we are able to connect better as a result of that commonality we share and believe in. This is the power of commonality. You cannot succeed in anything with anyone, if you do not share similar attentions. Or best put, you will hardly succeed with someone if you do not share similar values.

FOOD FOR THOUGHT:

Regardless of any answers suggested by various respected personalities through my research, it remains their views, and yours remain yours, as opinions differ from person to person. Every situation presents itself differently, and it will depend on the circumstances that surround it to determine what to do. The context in which a situation is presented to you determines the action to take, even though some are obvious. It is easy to sit and analyze a situation presented in front of you, but things may be different when the reality is in front of you.

CHAPTER 20

Effective Listening and Its Impact on Commonality

We, many a time, confuse hearing with listening, and within the world of listening, we have effective listening. For the purposes of this study, let's assume listening connotes effective listening. Listening, in this case, goes beyond hearing. It is about paying close attention with the intent to understand, while hearing is about acknowledging what is being said but not necessarily paying attention to it.

For the purposes of this study, let's assume listening connotes effective listening. Listening in this case goes beyond hearing. It is about paying close attention with the intent to understand, while hearing is about acknowledging what is being said but not necessarily paying attention to it.

Unfortunately, not many people do this correctly. There are people who form a preconceived notion about someone, and whatever that person may say or do would not change it. There is the flip side where another person says anything, regardless of the tone and timing, it is regarded as the best idea, even if it isn't.

We live in a world where you need to earn a reputation and respect in order for people to even listen to you. Being in conversation is just being there in body and presence but not necessarily with the mind. To satisfy someone, people sometimes stay in conversation but never pay attention. That is why you see people congregated somewhere with the assumed intent to listen to a speech, but after the speech, if you ask people what was exactly said, I believe probably, only about twenty percent of the group could articulate what they had heard, thirty percent of that same group may try to pull it together for you but may not be accurate, while the remainder fifty percent may not be able to say anything at all, probably just a word or two.

This happens in any form of gathering, including political events, churches, mosques, workplaces and many more.

When I was interviewed for my first job after grad school, I was privileged to be interviewed by about seven senior executives in the company. During the conversation with a prominent senior executive, I was able to turn the interview around by asking him what made him successful and how he got to where he was (obviously I wanted to learn and go beyond some day). And all he said was, "I paid attention to detail". I have always remembered that statement and applied it thoroughly throughout my career because he was a successful man and who was open-minded, trustworthy, and ready to share. That was a man who never gave up on me in spite of many challenges I went through because he believed in my capabilities. He saw a level of fighting spirit and future in me, and he was ready to invest in a person who was willing to listen but at the same time not just be a "yes sir" person. People sometimes mistake respect for weakness.

Don't let distractions keep you away from your destiny because there are many distractions and noises out there. One of the ways to catch a raccoon is to distract it by showing it a shiny object. People know what your distractions or shiny objects are, so they will play on your weakness to put you off-track. It may be intentional or unintentional, but whatever it is, the damage ends up on you.

In most parts of certain societies, you need to be aggressive, challenge everyone, and be outspoken to be regarded as a smart person. The irony is that even if that person doesn't say things right or listens, the fact that he or she speaks always is enough to earn the desired recognition. How effective is this? I can't tell but it works for people and it is accepted. There are people who bark but never bite, and some who bark and actually bite. Some of these principles I can't make sense of, but I've learned also that if you're in Rome, do what the Romans do, so it is advisable to adapt but do not adapt towards what is negative. Make sure you adopt only those things that would add value to your life, and which make sense. There is no correlation between loud people and smart people. Those who talk but have no substance to back it are like those who bark and never bite. The opposite is those who talk and could produce results and are intelligent are like those who bark and know what they are talking about. Above all, listens.

Those who bark and know what they are talking about are the pruned people, and when they speak, you want to listen to them because they practice what they preach.

Listening is more than just paying attention to what is being said; you need to watch and listen to nonverbal cues as well.

"The most important thing in communication is listening to what isn't said,"

- Peter Drucker.

Imagine having a conference phone conversation with a trusted friend, but while the conversation is ongoing, your partner enters the room. This trusted friend is suggesting something to do for which your partner is a subject matter expert. You immediately place the call on speaker-phone so your partner can hear what is being said on the other side. What your trusted friend is suggesting doesn't make your partner comfortable at the time, so instead of immediately saying you aren't comfortable, you go ahead to affirm your friend's suggestion, but while speaking, you gave your partner a gesture by looking him or her in the eyes, signaling your finger and shaking your head, depicting that you weren't going to do what your friend was suggesting. In this case, who is speaking louder? The words of affirmation or the nonverbal clues and signs you are giving to your partner? The spoken word to the hearing of everyone, or the signal? Obviously, the latter. You can listen with your eyes through eye contact combined with body language. You can also listen by watching someone's disinterest through scratching of his face, yawning, partly paying attention, or ignoring you even though physically present.

In this world that we live in, there are people who make judgments and form opinions about other people based on what they hear from their colleagues. They are unable to take a stance or decide for themselves regarding what they believe in. This may be because of a lack of self-confidence, or it may also be because by so doing, they might win the hearts of their peers for selfish gains.

These types of people are dangerous people to begin with, they are usually in the form of balloons that are blown in any direction that the air dictates and they obey. They have no stance on their own but live their lives on the shoulders of other people's opinions or what they want to hear, not what is being said. They have no opinion themselves. You need to stay far away from such people. You will not have any positive relationship with them, so don't even create the environment to suggest so, unless there is a proven change. You may be forced to see these people because they are the same people with whom you go to work or school with, they may be your neighbors, or they do something in common (not to be confused with commonality) with you, but you can still stay away mentally. For such people, time will tell when you may have to detach yourself from them physically, but in the meantime, train your mind to stay away. We only have life once on earth, and it must be lived to the fullest satisfaction with the right people. It's just a matter of time.

You may be with them physically, but do not be there with your mind. You need to be careful what you say and what you don't say. What you don't say may even be louder than what you do say. People in this category will always desire to know what is in your mind to be able to manipulate you because they are not certain and not sure of themselves. They are always looking for weaker ones to measure with. These are people who see their superiors as gods and will do anything possible to please them by throwing others under the bus to gain what they aspire to, be it position, recognition, award, or friendship.

I am suggesting that most great people who work hard and are genuine and who are awarded and do the right thing fall under this category. Stay away from the former, both mentally and psychologically. Some try to listen to please their bosses, lecturers, and friends just to mention few; however, we need to do it in a way that is mannered and acceptable. Some believe in adhering to the truth, and so will tell it like it is, but others will always condone what is evil to gain momentary praise. You're not to be known as the striker for every scenario all the time. In other words, don't always be the first to speak if you don't have to. People wrongly enjoy the praise for calling things the way it is without applying wisdom to the statement. Saying it well and at the right time is what will carry weight and create positive listening power with the right effect.

If you're endowed with some unique talent and wisdom and for some reason you decide not to use it, it will decay over time and be taken away from you. If you possess such talent but are unwilling to share it with the world, very soon it would be made redundant because people would catch up or that same talent will be granted to another person as an opportunity to be of help, making you seem inept. This is what happens when people presume the world revolves around them due the fact that they still possess the same power they had over people some years ago on account of their level, position, or previous opportunities. Oh, sorry soul, people have moved on long ago. Wake up from your dreaming slumber.

You make a name not just by helping those who are already smart, excellent, and have a clear future, but you make a name by helping the destitute and hopeless, and redefining someone's life.

The movie 'Troy' comes to mind. When the young messenger came to inform the lead actor, Troy about his next opponent, the boy was so terrified that he described to Troy how huge and massive this opponent was, how strong, gigantic, and fearful he was, and the fact that he hadn't seen anything like him before.

Troy looked at him, ruffled his fingers through this young messenger's hair, and said to him, "Oh, boy, this is why your name is not written in any book." Then he left on a horse straight to the battlefield to conquer this giant.

You need patience, self-sacrifice, dedication, and an open mind to help someone. I am proud to have come across people who believed in me when others, unfortunately, did not, sometimes because of their personal agenda. They did this selflessly and sometimes defend my position when I was not there. I came to know some of this just by sheer coincidence. There are people who do things to claim human praise sometimes for selfish reasons, for promotion, for certain unexplained gains. However, there are others who do things just for the love of it, regardless of who sees it or not. I love the latter because they are less dangerous and could go all the miles for you when the time comes.

FOOD FOR THOUGHT:

There is a reason why we have two ears and one mouth. This is an indication that you listen more and talk less. Do not just listen with your ears but also with your heart. Show interest in people when they are talking to you or sharing importing information with you. It heals, it's respectful, it builds trust, it's convincing, it's a blessing, and it's good practice. When listening, pay attention to what is actually being said to you, not what you think is being said. Do not jump to conclusions before a sentence is complete, as you may misunderstand and misrepresent the entire story. That could also affect the sort of answer you may provide. This is even more crucial when you are a leader.

CHAPTER 21

Some Uniquely Identified Ways to Find Commonality

There are ways one can find commonality among people. Commonality can be found with people based on many factors that are of interest to you, however, it is also important to identify the best approach.

Below are some of the identified areas of commonality;

COMMON INTERESTS:

Finding shared interest and passion for something is a fantastic way to identify like-minded souls. Whether a passion or interest be for reading, sports, food, or even more obscure hobbies, these commonalities will bring the opportunity to share knowledge and ideas, which will strengthen the bond you have with a person.

"Hopefully, someday we will both realize that despite our sharp differences, you and I have more in common than we think."

- Ray Bourhis, Revolt: The Secession of Mill Valley

COMMON EXPERIENCES:

Experiences stem from our senses and tap into our emotions. To share an experience with someone is to share some of the same connections in the brain. People who work in demanding professions, such as journalism, consulting and entrepreneurship as an example, know this too well, and often find themselves socializing with others who have experienced the same stresses and joys that they have.

COMMON BELIEFS AND VIEWS:

Shared beliefs also bond people and connect them at a high level. A Jew would feel more at home with another Jew, and the same applies to a Hindu, a Christian, and similar to a Veteran who served in the same mission. This is simply so because conversation and understanding are easier among people with the same faith and beliefs compared to if they were not. Their interests are obviously mutual, and so their interaction needs less explanation. While great friends are still made across the board, it is possible only among mature minds. For instance, I have many Muslim friends even though I profess Christianity. It is not so easy for everyone. Naturally, common faith and beliefs bond people more closely as, arguably, they leave less room for misunderstanding between people.

COMMONALITY IN MARRIAGE:

A lot of marriages fall apart because of a lack of understanding and simple acts of maturity like changing small habits (like not leaving your socks in your shoes) for each other. Marriage doesn't work when nobody wants to shift and everyone wants to stay in his or her position.

Some people want to lead the same life that they were used to prior to marriage, and we all know that's absolutely impossible. Until there is a sense of commonality and the fact that we all need each other and are willing to accept each other's faults and work on them, there will always be a separation—at least mentally if not physically. There are so many people who are mentally and emotionally divorced from each other, but for the sake of their friends and society or for their children, force themselves to continue living together. They may engage in sexual practice, but the mind may be somewhere far off. I hope this stops, and people become better able to find a common ground to relate.

SOME UNIQUELY IDENTIFIED WAYS TO FIND COMMONALITY

Commonality may come naturally (we both happen to like sports) but it also required change or deliberate act (like me learning to like football). In marriage the same principle applies, we get into a relationship because of what we have in common, but we keep it going because of what we are willing to sow, new habits and the like, to support friendship or marriage.

"Stop trying to explore what is different about yourselves and explore the commonality you have instead."

- René Gaudette

WORKPLACE COMMONALITY AND OTHER RELATED DILEMMA:

When a company is interviewing a candidate for a job, what they are often actually looking for is the spirit of commonality or fit before talent. If you are intelligent but they find no fit, your chances of getting that position are slim, unless the competition is less. If you happened to have been chosen under special circumstances, note that your main orientation for the set period would be customized for fit. To be fit for a position comes with so many other elements that may not necessarily be written down. How you talk, how you behave, if it is a lunch meeting, how you eat, etc. The recruiter's job is to get it right, and the people they bring into the workforce would reflect that recruiter's decision.

The lens from which everyone sees things differs from individual to individual. This is based on people you surround yourself with, where you were born, what you read, your associations, the schools you attended, the religious group you belong to, arguably what you eat, and so on. Exposure is the enemy of narrow-mindedness. While it is good to be exposed in order to broaden one's mind, it is what you learn and do with that exposure that counts most.

I am privy to every situation in my life's path. I have seen enough of the world and worked in various institutions all over the globe. I have worked with faith-based leaders and ordinary people. I have also worked with the rich and the poor. I have worked with people who are hypocrites but pretend they are not, the rude and also the humble, etc. I have worked with leaders who desire the best by pointing people to the right side, but when the gavel is pointing at them, would not accept it. This is simply because the rules are affecting them personally so they will find any means to turn it off in their favor. Probably, the rules were made for others, not them nor their families. I have as well lived and visited rich countries and know certain places that are poor which all form the cradle of my life.

I had a boss who was at the time successful in his style of leadership. In other words, he was at the peak of his career. He was very respected and honored at all times. It was at the earliest stage of my career, so I was much younger and less experienced.

I recall during one of my visits to this man's nice and classy office at the time, we were having our usual update chats (it is good to note that a lot of protocols and months of bookings and rebooking's had taken place to get on his schedule). One of my queries to him was why was it that whenever I suggested something to my senior management, they didn't take it. This was frustrating to me. The reason I asked was that, coincidentally, after ignoring my suggestions, in a few months, this same man that I was talking to, who was then our senior-most global leader, would come and say something similar in his suggestions to the department, and they would applause and accept with glee. I was dumbfounded most of the times this happened. He said in a polite answer to me, *"Evans, relax. Keep working hard and continue to pay attention; it is because you haven't earned it yet. When that time comes, you'll understand it."* In fact, I didn't quite understand then what he meant, but over time, I got it. Indeed, after taking time, learning, reading, paying attention, and doing all the needed things but more critically, observing through experimentation, I truly got it and I appreciate him for what he said to me.

It is said that on the day you are born, both your angels and enemies are born with you, so it will depend on the paths you take in life and the decisions you make to shape your future that will determine which one dominates over you. I am always positive in spite of the many challenges. Did I get angry and walk out of this man's office? No. I don't think I would have learned anything. I also don't think he would have opened his office doors again for me to seek advice. I continued to pursue his attention until I got promoted.

This leader at the time had brought many people into the institution—people he had previously worked with over the years and who had high powered leadership positions. Not only this, those leaders had also brought people they too were comfortable with, whether they were good or bad, qualified for the position or not, they came. This only goes to explain the system of camaraderie in the world setting. You may be as smart as a whip, but if you have nothing in common with anyone, your next step may be steep. This is no different from most politicians who recruit their friends, not necessarily because they are the most talented people they know but because they are comfortable with them, and for some reason, speak the same language they do in terms of career, education, sports, belief system, policies, and many other related issues.

Talking about language, someone who speaks French, for example, regardless of color of the skin, will connect with another person who speaks French because they have something in common. I was on one of the advisory boards that I am privileged to have served on, and during the happy hour meeting that was organized with many people, something strange happened. I had gotten in early with another colleague whom I served on another board with. We both came in early due to an earlier commitment that we had prior to coming there. We had a good time connecting with many new and old people, exchanged pleasantries over a drink, but when it was time to retire, I walked over to a young lady who had come in late. All I did was introduced myself and mentioned where I originally came from. It was as if I had released the chicken from the coop. This lady jumped and hugged me and started screaming with overexcitement. I was feeling good, thinking she might have come from my place too, but guess what, she had only visited that country for a short time, but knew all the dances and their names, the names of all the critical regions, the food, the people, and had even started demonstrating one of the tribes' dances to me right then and there. This experience electrified our relationship instantly, and we became strong pals thereafter. It took the power of commonality for that fire to light naturally.

COMMONALITY WITH THE RICH:

Rich people are more likely to relate to each other as friends far more than to the poor. This is not correlated to the charity work that they do with low-income communities, since that is a different type of relationship. Relating with each other is different and simple as they are able to golf together, eat at unique and expensive places together, meet each other at high-class events, fly first-class if they are not in their private jets, talk about the schools they had attended, and so on. They are able to discuss and sign contracts and give each other opportunities that serve them best. How can any other class of person fit in?

COMMONALITY WITH THE POOR:

On the flip side, just as it is easier for the rich to connect with the rich, people with low-income share common goals in terms of where they live, where they meet, schools they had attended, and so on. They meet on the bus, the market, cheap shops, and such venues that are common to them. They too find the same commonality to connect with each other. They sometimes communally gossip about the rich and how they are not supporting them as they should. That's what brings them together; it is their commonality.

CROSS-LINE COMMONALITY:

This is where someone may be poor and raised in a totally different environment, but due to education and the talent he or she may have had and been exposed to, would be able to relate, eat, befriend, and roll in the circles of the rich, or at least certain circles. Such a person may be gifted in something others may not possess, which could be a special talent. This, as a result, gives him or her the natural right and opening to live like never before.

Because someone has a lot of travel experience and relates to another group of people who also share similar adventures, even if not necessarily the same places, the fact that they share the same mindset would serve or grant as a connection somehow. The fact that someone or a group of people wear a particular dress or buy from a particular place, one way or the other artificially embraces them to start a conversation. *"Where did you get yours?" "How did you get it?"* This makes both groups or persons see each other as coequals. How one turns that into a positive connection for a life-changing experience depends entirely on the person in question. Who needs whom most in this case?

Taking Action:

Talking of finding common grounds, it is important to note that the seemingly little things matter. Roaring success may not be assured instantly on the sheer account of commonality. Concrete solidification of links calls for the test of time and requires lots of deliberate energy to achieve. When, however, this foundation had been laid strongly, it bears the heavy demands, which the relationship calls for. Once it is valued, therefore, one should take time and pay the needed attention required for creating and maintaining such links in one's life. As much as common ground lends much to the relationship, it is not enough if one really wants to preserve the link.

In his article, "Finding Commonalities and Common Ground Fast," John E. Kobara stated:

"All of us have stories about discovering amazing things we have in common with people we just met or have known for a long time. You find out that you both went to the same high school, share a hobby, your parents know each other, and you have a close friend in common.... A moment that reinforces how increasingly small the world is. What if we could figure out those connections sooner? Knowing how our worlds overlap and intersect will only expedite the relationship and ultimately the trust between the parties".

Health issues, prison experiences, fighting for similar causes, love for a particular pet, and walking the dogs are some of the examples of areas in which one may share things in common.

South Africa, like many other nations, has gone through a lot with respect to freedom-fighting and the desire to lead their own affairs. Freedom fighters like Nelson Madiba Mandela (earlier mentioned), who had been their leader during the Apartheid era, fought and refused to come to an agreement because there was no common ground to stand on. The white South Africans believed they deserved the land, while the blacks naturally believed the land was theirs. It took a lot of bloodshed, prison terms, and serious fights amongst the groups until 1990 when, after releasing Nelson Mandela from prison, that the opportunity for democracy presented itself. Nelson Mandela had to pay the price of his entire prime and youthful life as sacrifice for his nation's freedom, and later became the first black president. Mandela also nominated in modern times his two main opposition leaders from other political parties and beliefs to work with him as his presidential deputies—Frederick De Clerk and Thabo Mbeki. This was one of the rarest and wisest decisions I have come across ever since the wisdom of King Solomon. Mandela tried to focus on the commonality between them rather than the differences they may have. He was acknowledging that they all loved their country and wanted the best for their people. This way, peace, to a very large extent, was enjoyed, wisdom was on display, and knowledge was shared. In order to lead the nation they all proclaimed they loved so much, he brought them along so they had to do it together. They had to find a common ground, and the peace and love they had for the nation and its progress was realized, instead of their war.

FOOD FOR THOUGHT:

Without a common denominator, there is no way you can have a common ground or commonality with anyone. What is your common denominator? You will need to know yours and let others see or know theirs too. That is the only way to connect. If you are a good dancer, it is only when you are on the dance floor that people would applaud and admire you, not when the government needs political decisions and is in the middle of global negotiations. If you are a sports hero, like Usain Bolt or Roger Federer or Serena Williams and the like, you are only recognized during the times you demonstrate your expertise or talent at the right time. Until then, you are just another human being, though a celebrity. You will probably enjoy some recognitions depending on the height of your celebrity, but your glorious moments are when you are on top and in action. Consider this: During the historic inauguration of former President Barack Obama as the first African American into the highest office of the free world, there were many celebrities who attended the occasion. Singers, sports icons, politicians (of course), authors, inventors, and businessmen and women were all present. But the spotlight was on the new celebrity in town, the President, so they did not receive any special cheers from the public. However, give them their stage and another time, and the screams of the public would wake you up.

* * *

CHAPTER 22

How to Use the Power of Commonality Positively

It is one thing identifying with someone with a common purpose, and another positively taking advantage of the situation to build a relationship. It is important to note that this is not automatic but needs some form of skills to get connected. I have learned over the years through education and observation that having riches or knowing people and people knowing you back is just a step; maintaining them is the most important thing.

I know a lot of people who know people in high places, and in fact, people of different positions, backgrounds, and the like. They have dozens of business cards of such people stuck and overflowing in their boxes.

I know some who boast of the fact that they have acquaintance with special people who hail from their native country or hometown, or even had lunch with them before. Some go the length of showing you instant pictures they might have taken with some of these great people.

I don't intend to be mean, but my reaction is usually, *"So what?"* I am genuinely excited to see all that; however, I see such as only a first step. What is more important is whether they also know you back. Would such dignitaries have similar reaction(s) about you when your name is mentioned? Would your image be immediately clear in their mind when you're mentioned? How do they know you? What impact have you made in their lives? Have you done anything positive and unforgettable that they may remember you by? Would your first name pop up in their mind when your last name is mentioned?

SYNERGY AND COMMONALITY

Someone once narrated to me how he had the opportunity to work with a very important senator in Nigeria. According to him, he had met a perpetual drunkard somewhere in Nigeria, and circumstances had made them live together. One day, he told this drunk that he wished to meet a senator to gain some promotion in life. Immediately, this drunk mentioned this senator and advised him to go and see him. How was he, a common struggler in Nigeria, able to make this senator pay him any attention? The drunkard told him once he met the senator, he should say it was he, *"Olu Two,"* who had sent him. This friend of mine did not take the man seriously, but he chose to go to Abuja, their capital, just to try his luck.

To his surprise, when he met the senator and mentioned Olu Two, this great man turned with rapt and eager attention to him. *"Where did you meet Olu Two?"* he asked with grave concern. It turned out that the drunkard had been very close to the senator and played many positive roles in his life, so the very mention of his name was enough to earn him a job with the senator who later told him much about Olu Two whom he clearly cherished very much except for his excessive drinking lifestyle.

What are we learning here? That was a drunkard deemed useless but for the fact that he was once good to this man, so his name alone could elicit positive spontaneous response from such a great man.

The point here is reciprocity is crucial in every relationship. Your reciprocity may be just how you respect time, or the fact that you are someone imbued with integrity, hence are trustworthy, your intelligence, your grace, how you carry yourself, your eloquence, your listening power, your humility, how you fight for others with passion, never asking for anything even when it is obvious you need it. This and many more could attract someone's permanent attention to you in return, which you may never know.

Building relationships takes not just a photo or rushing for business cards, but also connecting with the person in such a way that would always make you memorable.

During my college days, I was blessed to be among the first supply chain management students at the time that was awarded graduate assistantship in that department, and so was privileged to have collated and seen different types of resumes and different approaches in an attempt to land a great job. This was made possible because as part of the assistantship, I needed to work in the office of one of the professors. As a result of what I was privileged to see, in terms of diverse resumes that poured into the office, I was determined to be different in creating mine to stand out. I was so determined to write mine differently that I came up with a very unique strategy, whereby I really made my resume stand out because I had seen it all—the best and the worst. As a result, I had many Fortune 500 companies throwing invitations to me to come for an interview. Some of such respected institutions invited me mainly due to the structure and content of my resume. I was flown to many companies across the United States, and one that I vividly remember was in Cisco in Silicon Valley, for example, one of the interested companies in me. Though I didn't get the job, I was later informed by a reliable source who was then a staff that my invitation was mainly due to how my resume was structured, the numbers therein, the percentages, the layout, the wording, its crispness, how easy it was to read, how straight to the point it was, how I wisely crafted both the responsibilities and achievement elements therein, and most importantly, answered the question most employers silently have, like the *"and so what's?"* part, which most people missed. For example, instead of just stating or writing, *"I was in charge of the institution's financial portfolio,"* I went further or would rather say, *"I was in charge of the company's financial portfolio within the period of my leadership, which led to an X US Dollars savings of X amount."* The latter was smarter and crisper, answering the *"and so what?"* part by telling the story of what it led to, rather than leaving it vague. I used keywords like 'crafted', 'developed', 'managed', 'successfully', 'innovated', plus the most attractive and accepted jargon to get what I wanted.

In other words, I got the companies attracted to me due to the sheer peculiarity of my resume. In addition to the uniqueness of my resume at the time, I had timelines in it. In the end, I received the tag of *"Mr. Profile Man,"* due to the fact that whenever I went for interviews, I carried along a prepared profile, well-packaged and bonded, which included high level (30,000 foot) summary that detailed and enforced most of the statements of achievements mentioned in my resume. This included but was not limited to the processes I used in achieving those numbers, the results and from which company. I was very smart about my resume and probably the only candidate at the time that adopted this strategy. It worked for me. Oh boy, I stood out. Whenever the interviewer attempted to ask anything in line with what I had, I immediately shared the detailed content but in a very

SYNERGY AND COMMONALITY

slick and crisp manner through the profile, in terms of how it was done, which included pictorials, graphs, and layouts, including quick and easy-to-understand images.

One of the vivid approaches was a particular cycle I managed to adopt that reduced process duplication, which was part of my project work in one of the big institutions in Richmond Virginia, reducing from a standard forty five days to a revised thirty five days, saving nine to ten days, thereby leading to millions of dollars in savings both in time (opportunity cost) and in US dollar terms. In simple terms, every day in the corporation brought in millions of US dollars also because those extra days could be used for other alternative opportunities, and when accumulated year over year, would lead to a savings of many weeks and months.

One positive warning I always had in my heart for prospective employers was, *"If you invite me for an interview, you'd better believe that I will win the job!"* That was not the case at Cisco. Someone better was hired. I am humble enough to state that the person who eventually succeeded over me might be an extremely gifted genius. I would like to meet that person just to shake his or her hand and say, *"Well done!"* I was not being cocky; I simply had confidence in myself and in how well I had prepared to be the best in whatever I did, and do.

Sometimes people are ahead of their time in terms of how they think, how they work, their ideas, and how forward-looking they are. If they don't have similar types of people around them, they are misunderstood but later appreciated when they are no longer there.

I recall one of the major gatherings of the Institute of Supply Management (ISM) in Las Vegas. This was during my MBA days when I was amongst the few students and leaders (because I served as a student leader then) who were invited to be part of such an event. At the time, a major institution for an internship was recruiting me. Other institutions were also in attendance, both for the conference itself and to seek talented students for major hires and internships. These were students from various recognized institutions across America and beyond.

I recall a particular meeting where both students and senior leaders from all the major companies were introducing themselves. One of the respected executives representing a giant company introduced herself first and then her company (which was a well-known institution), and then, without warning, she pointed in my direction and stated emphatically: *"And please, no one touch Evans Mensah. He is ours and coming to work with us!"*

Everyone turned, looked at me, and started laughing with admiration. What an advertisement for me! What she did, little did she know, was to create many opportunities for me later. She contributed to my life's success, no matter how small that gesture might have seemed. It was more than an endorsement. This was the institution that I used in my profile, mainly. Interestingly, that statement or open endorsement caused many other leaders who hadn't known me to chase after me, as people wanted to know who I was for someone like her to lay such an authoritative claim on me. I believe this wonderful lady (Regina she was called) wanted to send a straight message, as she had seen some executives talking to me even prior to the meeting. Ironically, by then I was sitting next to one of the most respected executives from another company who was chatting with me and who had intentionally asked that I sit next to him. This was the man who later became the board chair of ISM and hired me six to seven months prior to my graduation from college, and was the one I was referring to when he asked me to pay attention to detail. The recognition made a huge impact on me. It wasn't that I was the best in the crowd or had the best solution to anything. After all, they'd never had the opportunity to test me. I was simply favored, and it was my season. Nevertheless, good preparation via my carefully prepared resume also deserves some of the credit. I always stress the importance of preparing well ahead of every battle and challenge. No sloppy venture succeeds except by accident.

In the many business cards I gave and received, one thing I have always done and continue to do is to write on the back the date I met the person and any details or information that would help me to remember and easily recall how we met. Usually, we take things for granted and just take and keep those cards somewhere, believing we will always remember. After about six months, we are scratching our heads as to who that person is, where we must have met him or her, who had introduced that person to us. To avoid such embarrassing situations, I practice the above as soon as possible, if not immediately. Make it a habit to exercise the same.

FOOD FOR THOUGHT:

Don't look down on anyone by the virtue of how they look, talk, dress or where society might have placed them. You should also treat people with respect as your angel might be next to you. And know that, beyond talents and skills are also buried the values of honor, integrity, credibility and how you position yourself in society to be seen positively.

CHAPTER 23

Creating and Attracting a Sense of Commonality

The choices we make in life depend on our surroundings most times, so it is good to make the wise choices.

Be yourself: Unless you are on the wrong path, refine who you are, but do not change who you are. The day you try to be someone else might be the same day someone may be seeking to know that person in you, and you would have missed the opportunity

Win: Winning involves doing whatever you need to do well and doing it better than your competition. Competition, in this case, isn't always amongst company to company; the next person near you can be considered a competitor. Learn to think ahead of your generation: Create *"aha"* moments by being proactive rather than reactive. Always think about tomorrow before taking any action today. Winning also naturally draws people to you, and in the process, you can select who fits best to your need at the time.

Surround Yourself with the Right People: The decision to be positive or negative, to succeed or to fail, to go to school or not, to learn a trade or profession, to have the right attitude or not, depends on the type of people you surround yourself with. You cannot do anything about your family's make up, in terms of who your father or mother or siblings should be, but you can choose to distance yourself from toxic members of your family. You can, however, choose your friends, but remember whoever you choose to align with will greatly influence the type of lifestyle you will have. If you choose friends who love education, you'll value education and choose activities accordingly. If you make friends with people who love to party, expect to be partying all the time. It is therefore important to be careful about whom you decide to associate with, as that may be the image that will follow you for the rest of your life.

Food and Choices: A vegetarian is more likely to speak the same language of food with another vegetarian than someone who loves meat. Regardless of one's belief, the choices we make comes with its consequences. The choice of elected public officers who either come to help or mess the system has its consequences on us. The choice of whom we marry has its own consequences. Not different from the type of food we choose to eat. Regardless of what type of choices we make, be it food or anything, people relate to you much better or share the same affiliation with you because you have something in common.

Caution:

Rather than seeking to be a people pleaser, use your conscience to judge what is right and stick to it. If you become a people pleaser, you risk turning into a robot and not using your brains. Recall the horrific story of Jonestown in the 1970s, where a spiritual leader, Jim Jones, convinced thousands of followers to kill themselves by drinking poison. You have a brain, and you need to use it wisely. In that way, in the process of trying to relate with someone or a group of people, make sure they are going to be a good influence. Go beyond what you see and seek extra knowledge.

THE BANK EXPERIENCE:

One day my wife went to a popular bank where we had an account in order to conduct some notary business; however, the waiting time was a bit too long. The young lady at the desk politely said the wait would be at least thirty minutes because they were dealing with a lot of wedding-related issues. That was the first time I knew banks were also involved in wedding stuff in terms of notaries and the like. My wife then politely thanked the banker and left to check out another bank nearby, as she didn't have time to wait that long, knowing those thirty minutes could easily turn out to be an hour.

When my wife entered the next bank (where we did not currently have an account), she met a beautiful woman at the door who struck up a conversation with her immediately. They both engaged in a hearty chat as though they'd known each other for years.

This woman in this bank happened to be the branch manager. She was ready to assist my wife with anything she needed for free, and as efficiently and proficiently as possible. She even alluded that, in the future, whatever my wife might need, she was ready to support her and the children. I was not mentioned, obviously left out of the party—too bad for me. There were specific items and a particular type of identification they might need, but the branch manager said that even though other banks—and even hers—would have to get those items, she was prepared to assist my wife based on trust. My wife got everything she needed at the time for free, got the bankers business card, and promised to stay in touch.

As a result, we ended up opening new accounts and transferring our existing account from the other bank into this new one. This same lady met me in line one time while I was holding a folder, if I recall properly. She asked what I was holding, and I mentioned to her I needed to fax something after my transaction. She immediately took the folder, got the fax number, and sent the fax for me. By then I was done with my transaction, and she vanished without allowing me extra space to say thanks. This is the character of this person, and our treatment also probably had something to do with the fact that we were polite to her, always saying thank you and asking questions the average person wouldn't ask. She felt valued and cared for, and so did we.

The power of commonality works and cannot be taken for granted, but how it is used depends on the individual. This banker became the reason we moved all of our accounts from one bank to hers. What a powerful marketing tool her kindness and helpfulness was!

There are many people who are blessed with opportunities to take advantage of commonality, but because the opportunity doesn't come in the form and shape they might have expected, they turn it down. Life is not always about money. In fact, life is richer if you focus on living well and treating others, as you would like to be treated.

FOOD FOR THOUGHT:

A lot of businesses are losing clients because of a lack of simple etiquette. On the other hand, some businesses are growing because they do the right things. Creating a consistent culture across your organization is one of the best ways to attract people to you. It pays to be nice whether in person or on the phone. Tips are given because of the unique service someone receives, and usually, the better the service, the greater the tip. Customer service is key if you want to maintain or increase your client base. That will lead to more profits and increased market share, and you can also expect most customers to stick with you in difficult times. Teach it, train your workers and live by what you say.

CHAPTER 24

Perception or Ignorance?

Perception has played and continues to play a huge role in the minds of so many people. Incorrect perception is blocking most people slowly from arriving at the truth, as a result, not expanding on opportunities probably meant for them. Why should you think everyone with an accent, especially an accent from a third-world country, is poor? Yes, poverty certainly does exist in those countries or continents, but some people are living extremely well, and it is wrong to use a segment to draw a conclusion about everyone.

When it comes to having an accent, it is funny because an accent in itself is relative. A New Yorker visiting California will be perceived to have an accent because the former speaks faster compared to the latter and some intonations are different. Most westerners who move to a new location will be described as having an accent, but it's not usually seen in a negative light. However, the accent of someone from India, Latin America, Mexico, Africa or the like usually is met with hostility. This is sad and creates a narrow way of looking at things. Only when someone travels or is exposed to things outside of where they originally live would their mindset change. I know a segment of people in particular, though they are successful in their fields of work, they are very limitedly in their understanding of people who come from other parts of the world. Anytime they approach such people, they always presume they are doing them a favor—a favor to be their friend, a favor to talk to them, a favor to call them, a favor to work with them, a favor to consider them as playmates. This is absurd. They sometimes refer to immigrants as people who are probably used to milking cows and exchanging animals for other goods and services (barter system). This could be done in a typical village somewhere, just as the indigenous Americans live in a certain way, which people may describe as primitive, but that's their way of life. That doesn't mean everyone lives like that. The fact that a selected program is aired on television does not constitute an entire society's way of life. I don't blame people who think like this, nor I assume they mean it in a derogatory manner. I think they are just ignorant and informed differently. Placing everyone in one soup is a big danger. Break that eggshell of perception, or else you may be narrowing your opportunities and thereby limiting your destiny because you overlook other people who may not look or sound like you.

Ignorance is a disease. The fact that two or more people have certain things in common does not mean it is positive or healthy. I've heard a lot of people, even the media sometimes, refer a segment of a particular continent to be a country. Africa is one such example. This rich continent is often depicted as a small village sitting on a mountain somewhere.

Africans are often mischaracterized as people who don't live in houses or have anything to eat. What I see as poverty is more to do with the mindset and attitude of people. While it is true that Africa, on the whole, lacks many amenities, it is, however, endowed with mineral resources. I also know of another side of Africa, which is not known to some. People send foreign currencies from Africa to their loved ones to assist them in the western world to either pay their rents, mortgages or even school fees without taking a student loan. Some come for hospital appointments and pay off all bills with cash and return. However, this is mostly never reported or known. This too is Africa.

It is not appropriate or fair to judge an entire continent negatively for the actions of one country or region within that continent. When anything happens in France, for example, it should be limited to France, or the French, not Europe.

I don't blame people too much because the media's misconception and misrepresentation of certain continents sends a wrong signal, and they contribute to this thinking. In this day and age, when the world is in our palms, when by a click of a button you can find any information you want, why not conduct some research yourself to truly know what the truth is? I see people land at certain airports with jungle boots on, thinking they were going to land in a jungle, only to feel isolated and odd.

PERCEPTION OR IGNORANCE?

You know one thing that is common regardless of where anyone lives? Everyone has the same blood in them, and it is red, not green. Everyone wants a better life. Everyone wants a better education. Everyone wants clean water, everyone wants the best for their children, and everyone desires a comfortable life. Every continent has different types of people—weird people, educated people, nice ladies, gentlemen, gays, different beliefs, atheist, politicians, opinion leaders, poverty, riches, and so on. Nothing is unique to any continent. Yes, some continents may have more than another, but there is a common thread that binds us together. Be exposed and relate!

I have seen people who applaud ideas of other people who sound and look like them, but when someone speaks differently, no matter what they say, it is not taken or considered as wise. I admire organizations like the United Nations where I currently serve as a National Council Member for its Association in the USA, and Chairing the Collaboration and Partnerships Committee (SDG 17). They give opportunity to anyone who deserves to succeed, to be on top, provided you have what it takes to be there. Imagine Secretary General's like Ban Ki-moon, (Korea), Kofi Annan, (Ghana), Boutros Boutros-Ghali, (Egypt), Javier Perez de Cuellar, (Peru), Kurt Waldheim, (Austria.), U Thant, (Myanmar, formerly known as Burma), Dag Hammarskjöld, (Sweden), Trygve Lie, (Norway), and even the current head António Guterres (Portugal). Most of them originate from other nations and continents with some having heavy accents, but were able to make it to the highest ladder as Secretary General of the UN. This applies to the World Bank as well.

All my life, I have prepared myself for disappointments and created a 'deep hole' that serves as a 'shock absorber'. Meaning, nothing really surprises me any longer. I used to worry when I experience bad things, but over time, it passes like wind over my head. I don't get worried about anything anymore that does not add value to my life.

When people are in need, they show the pithiest and the humblest of behaviors in front of you, but when it's time to deliver, or when they get what they want, they start acting as though you rather owe them. Such people have no Integrity as part of their lives.

FOOD FOR THOUGHT:

Having knowledge on where someone is at a point in life and getting closer to people can help you understand them better. It will reduce incorrect perception and ignorance. Give people the chance to succeed and rejoice when they do. Listen and read deeper into what they are saying and create deeper respect for their knowledge. Build relationships with every class of person, and if you own a company or are a leader in a major or small institution, do not just satisfy the minimum diversity requirements. Rather, make it a point to employ the best if they fit. Avoid negative perception. Eddie Murphy's 1988 iconic movie 'Coming to America' may be just a movie, but it depicts a true lifestyle of many from the other side of the world. Ironically it is also the source of a lot of stereotypes about Africa, however, it is a good example of how to live amongst everyone to make a better world.

CHAPTER 25

Mentors Versus Advisors

Mentors should not be confused with advisors. Real mentors serve, while advisors usually instruct and give you direction to either take it or leave it. Mentors get to know you as a person, understand you as a person, and walk with you all the way through. This way, they build a level of personal relationship with you to create a sense of respect and share views. Advisors, on the other hand, may also care and want to help you, but only limited to what they could offer in a short amount of time. Both advisors and mentors are great persons to have in your life, but it's important to understand the difference between them.

I have spent considerable time mentoring and advising many people across the globe. In all these, I separate my style to the need of the individual. There are some I mentor, while some I only serve as a consultant and advisor when needed. The more the individuals avail themselves, the more I avail myself to them. This usually goes to people I advise. With that said, there is always a bit of skepticism, carefulness, and measuring the allowance that you're being given and what you can take. However, with mentorship, I usually go the full length with someone. I am more personal and interested in every aspect of the person rather than just what brought us together. I am able to point out what needs to be done as we both analyze and discuss the options that are available. One thing I try to avoid is dictatorship. Though I am mentoring that person, I listen and allow them to talk. I use their own message, turn it, and then provide them with guidance in the best possible customized manner that would suit the particular situation.

Some people prefer to dictate to you, and if you don't take what they desire at a time, they neglect you and describe you as disrespectful and arrogant. In this day and age, knowledge has surpassed one's imagination. What many young people today are lacking is mostly direction, the right attitude, decision-making, and the right protocols needed to achieve a goal. Thinking that being old means being wise and expecting others to listen to you and not allow them to offer their own thoughts will make you out of place. Your thoughts need to be challenged constructively with good questions and answers. Even my young kids challenge me sometimes. To be honest, it is frustrating, but I always have to remind myself that this is the only way they could be smart and bold. Drop that quick temper and answer those questions as much as you can with humility. And don't be too proud to admit when you don't know the answer and will have to get back to someone. For all you know, the one asking you the question already has answers but wanted your opinion or just to test you.

There are times when what you say should be taken and would be. In that case, how you present it matters. There is always the encoding side of every message, which must go through the transmission meter, then most importantly, the decoding tunnel. What the recipient receives and understands matters a lot. Sometimes you may say something with a particular intended meaning; however it is decoded differently, and sometimes negatively. This usually happens in written communication. When that happens, change the mode of communication, reassess the situation, and learn to be humble. However, do not make 'fetish' out of your humility. Just be genuine about it. This is mentorship, not dictatorship.

I am blessed to be serving in the spaces as advisor, mentor, and consultant to many people and institutions, from executive coaching, to business strategy development, formally and informally. It is fascinating to know that, sometimes, your mentees can help you when you listen carefully to them. All you do is affirm and guide. I had the opportunity to provide such guidance to those who were my seniors at the workplace at some point, which usually occurs behind the scenes after work and weekends. During weekdays, however, we act normal. This never happens in a normal life where a superior identifies a talent in a subordinate for guidance, because of the structure of the organization, it may not be accepted in daylight. It is expected in natural sense that only the older, the grey-haired, the one higher than you is wise enough to guide, but that is not necessarily true. There are exceptions, and this happened to me. Don't misunderstand me. Those who are higher than you got there because they did something better (in good circumstances) and they know better than you, so learn from them. I am only indicating special cases where someone may not be at the top yet, but from all indications, that person is above his or her generation, obviously climbing up and wise enough to guide. The only difference between that person and the standard top person is the title and paycheck.

Mentors tell you what you need to know, listen to you, and they do not hesitate to apply wisdom to help you all the way. Advisors are a bit cautious, trying not to hurt your feelings, so they mold you to a path to make your own decision eventually. They come in as needed and sometimes forget the previous advice they gave you. Mentors keep their eyes on you and check in regularly. This does not mean you have to meet with your mentees every week, or even monthly or every six months. I know some executives who meet their mentors once a year, and the relationship is still very effective. It all depends on the stage you're in and what you're looking for. There are some who prefer the babysitting strategy, so give them milk until they can start eating solid food mentally.

In any of the above circumstances, be it a mentor or advisor, there should be some level of connection between the two parties to make it work. Manage the situation well and see it as a blessing to help others or be blessed. You never know, that person you are helping today may serve as your child's mentor in the future and open bigger doors for them. That might be your investment in your entire life, just by your name. Some of them might serve as a silent prayer partner whose dedication and prayer might save you from an accident or a bad occurrence without you knowing.

Learn the habit of doing good and be genuine about it when you do it. It is one thing to feel for someone, and another thing to fight for him or her.

My goal here is not to give a lecture on whether an advisor or mentor is better. They both are there to help you, so take advantage of their wisdom, learn from them, build a relationship, and make sure you give back. My aim is to at least provide the difference and share thoughts on some of the ways to be effective. It is also crucial to note that when others spend time to give back through mentorship or advising, make it a point to listen.

Listening is a key part in any relationship. The mentee should also avail him or herself to be coached and accountable, or else it will be difficult to attain any improvement in life.

You cannot go far without having the right people around you. You can only go fast but not far. Along the path of life, you will meet so many different people, with diverse characters and different ways of seeing things. It is up to you to determine which path is best for you. The crowd is not always right, so seeing a huge crowd running on a path does not mean it is always the right path. As a matter of fact, only the few and the courageous make unique decisions from the pack. We drive in cars today because somebody made a brave decision. We may not have people like the Wright Brothers who invented airplanes, which now can fly us around the world with ease. Where would computers, the Internet or other inventions be today? It took a different thought from someone to make it happen. Those are found in the minority few who decided to think differently, who got support from people whom you may never know about. There are so many quitters out there, and it is easy to join the club. It's not so easy to join the train of the wise innovators and people who make a difference in society. It is not convenient to be successful, and so many people who always want to live a comfortable life remain very average for the rest of their lives.

While a lot of people are scared of change and scared of the future, we should rather shape the future. This is why getting direction from the right source is very important in any step you take.

FOOD FOR THOUGHT:

For a mentor-mentee relationship to be successful, both parties need to work together for a common goal. The mentee should learn to relate and should be humble and coachable to be able to get all the assistance he or she needs.

Work your strength and hire your weakness. Remember, there is gold in all of us, but one needs strength and courage and, of course, the right people in your life to help you dig and find that gold. There are some who do all the above and only ends up at the digging stage, almost finding their gold but giving up at the end. Don't be in that category. Continue digging till you find your gold. Yours may be found earlier than others, but it doesn't mean you're better. You are probably simply using the right tool while others aren't. Imagine using a machete to cut a huge tree. How long will it take for that tree to fall, compared to someone using a chainsaw? Get advice and make sure you have the right tools to succeed in life.

BE THERE:

When an opportunity is given to you, it is only open for a small time. The augmented blessing in helping other people is that you never know who that person may become tomorrow.

You should be proud to be a part of someone's life. Your best authority is recognized when you give more than you receive. In any case, the opportunity you have today is not perpetual. Everyone has his or her moments and time to hold the bullhorn, so make sure you don't miss the opportunities you have today. The people you may have ignored might become the ones you will need to rely on tomorrow.

Time is precious for people, and when they decide to help you and you're not prepared to be helped, you make life much difficult for yourself. Time is the scarcest resource in life and needs to be managed and not wasted on people who are stubborn, rebellious, and not ready to listen to good advice. If you fall into that category, it is time to wake up, regroup, and make a conscious effort to move on. I am not saying to give up on people who are lost and who need it most. What I am trying to say is be wise about people who intentionally desire to ruin and damage you; they don't deserve your time. Some of the decisions may be tough for you to carry, but you will need to humble yourself for help and be able to help yourself.

Paul Pierce the hall of famer and former Boston Celtics basketball champion, confessed that he was a little rebellious against his coach initially. It was not until he recognized the bigger picture in his life that he turned things around. He humbled himself and went to the coach's office, made amends, and told him he was ready to play, listen, and be coached. His coach was excited because there was no way Paul wouldn't succeed if he was willing to be humble and allow himself to be coached. It was fascinating to watch when they shared these views during Paul's Hall of Fame day at Boston. With his team, they were able to win the championship in 2008. Paul recalls everyone who supported him and was there for him. An uncle believed in him and helped him create a wooden box in his backyard to practice making shots. An old pal supported him by practicing with him every day just to help him get better. He also had the support of his single mother, his teammates, and of course his wife and family. You always need someone there for you.

You will need to defeat the flouts in your life in order to push forward to succeed. You must overpower the negative, be positive, inspire yourself, and do not wait for anyone to motivate you to push forward. I have found myself in many situations where I needed to become my personal guide because my eyes were on the goal, and I was paying attention to the storms that surround me. Throughout my life, I have always been a fighter, not a quitter. Sometimes that has its negatives, but in most cases, it has helped and brought me to where I need to be today.

Despite our grieving, when a loved one passes away, like my parents, no one ever jumps into the tomb with them. People may cry uncontrollably and stand at the edge, but they eventually leave the loved one to be buried alone. What I am attempting to say is remember you need to love yourself, believe in yourself, and carve out your life to achieve whatever you want to achieve. As Dr. Martin Luther King, Jr. put it, *"If you can't fly, then run. If you can't run, then walk. If you can't walk, then crawl. But whatever you do, keep moving."*

A friend of mine used to tell me that if for some reason you cannot catch up with her, then she would meet you at the other side. People are bogged down with what is termed *"analysis paralysis."* They have so many ideas but cannot execute any. The ideas become so heavy that they don't know which one to execute, and for that reason, they end up not being able to do anything profitable in life. To put it best, they don't end up utilizing the full potential of their life. I have a quote from a respected man, Doug Luffborough, CEO of Luffborough & Associates. During an interview he said the following:

"Many young people live their lives watching their dreams being fulfilled through the lives of others with half the potential, half the skill set, half the education, half the home training, half the work ethic, and half the character; but because of negative influences and the people around them they have not been able to see the power and potential in their own lives. Therefore, other

people take what was intended for them. In order to go places other people aren't destined to go, you have to be willing to do the things other people aren't willing to do".

In fact, no one cares about your success as you do, so go the extra mile, work hard, and blend smart work with hard work. At the end of it all, listen and learn from those who have gone ahead of you, and be a better person.

The main takeaway here is no matter how good you are, you still need someone behind you as a guide, showing you where to go, and how to do it. You need someone to challenge you. When you are on your own, there is no accountability, so you can decide to do what you want to do at what time. It is not so when you have someone watching over you. The onus is on you to be humble enough to allow that person coach you. If you allow arrogance to play a part, you won't have a good result. Another important point to remember is that just because you might become richer than your coach does not give you the impetus to be a fool. Wisdom is not in how much you have in terms of money but rather how much you have in your brains and what you can do with it.

In addition, learn to be there for people, not for financial gains alone but for the availability of your wisdom and skills. And just as you do it for others, so will someone will be there for you too. The skills you possess to be there for someone may be redundant when you leave that sphere, as you will need someone else' skills to depend on.

CHAPTER 26

Free Brand Promotions

It is so fascinating when you see most of us promoting brands without knowing it. We wear polo shirts, hats, caps, pants, socks, etc. with brand logos and get nothing from it. Probably, just for the pride and emotional fulfillment. We have zero affiliation with those brands, but some people are practically ready to wait in long lines in freezing cold or even die for them. But why not think about promoting your personal brand? I am not saying there is anything wrong with it, but my perspective is we all have certain brands we like and will wear them to fit in and feel comfortable, but sometimes, one needs to start thinking differently. We have sports teams we adore and will do anything to support them. The same energy could be channeled to build your brand. Someone will ask, what brand? I don't have a company to promote. What I mean is simple. Why not wear your name on the back of your polo shirts? If you were called Mensah like me, wouldn't it be a great idea to wear Mensah 1 as the dad, Mensah 2 as the mom, Mensah 3 as the son or daughter, and so forth? If you have a charity you're involved in, why not promote that charity instead of a company you are promoting that you have no stake in. We become their billion-dollar walking advertisement with no direct affiliation whatsoever to them—for free. Actually, you pay them for it because you had to go to the shop and buy the item in order to then promote the brand for free when you wear it. People even go the length of buying banners and structures that they gain nothing from. It is about time to start changing our mindset and build some asset. In doing so, other people who may want to know more may inquire or do the same, and before you know it, you create a sense of camaraderie in that area, and you will start making a special impact. Imagine seeing people on the field wearing their name tags. All of a sudden, you will see people saying hello to each other because of the commonality of doing the same thing, thinking in the same direction, and having a sense of oneness. People will be forced to smile at each other because they seem to have a common purpose. This may hardly happen to someone wearing a Nike brand when they see another person in Nike because it is a mass production, nothing too special anymore. Unless that particular make or design is unique. In that case, you may receive some high fives or some sort of smile from the other person(s) wearing the same because of a level of class you belong, but that's it. However, my point is simple: it's better to create and build something you have direct impact on than the alternative. Once in a while, let's enjoy what we wear, but most times let's promote what we have and create a common point of connection between one another.

FOOD FOR THOUGHT:

The takeaway is to start thinking differently, or else someone will think for you. If you have an idea, build on it. I had a great business idea some time ago to create a windshield snow cover. I wanted to create it in such a way that all you do is clip the invention on top of your windscreen so that when it snows and you are in a hurry (for those who park their cars in the open), all you do is take it off, shake it, and get rolling. I sat on this idea for more than seven years, and before I knew it, someone else had invented it. That was a good lesson for me. Anytime I see that product, I respect the one who brought it to market. As painful as it may be, I don't get angry over it because I never pursued the vision. It is one thing having a great vision and another to work at it. I never took the needed step to achieve that aim. That's part of the reason I came back to write this book. Grow what you have!

✶ ✶ ✶

CHAPTER 27

One Body, Many Parts: A Metaphor for Life

Consider how the parts of the human body complement each other.

The eye is nothing like the head, but they need each other to see and think. The leg and the arm are two different things. The arm needs the leg to help it propel each other better. Let me borrow a verse in the Bible in 1 Corinthians 12 in the New International Version:

> *"Unity and Diversity in the Body"*
>
> *"Just as a body, though one, has many parts, but all its many parts form one body, so it is with Christ. For we were all baptized by one Spirit so as to form one body—whether Jews or Gentiles, slave or free—and we were all given the one Spirit to drink. Even so the body is not made up of one part but of many. Now if the foot should say, "Because I am not a hand, I do not belong to the body," it would not for that reason stop being part of the body. And if the ear should say, "Because I am not an eye, I do not belong to the body," it would not for that reason stop being part of the body. If the whole body were an eye, where would the sense of hearing be? If the whole body were an ear, where would the sense of smell be? But in fact God has placed the parts in the body, every one of them, just as he wanted them to be. If they were all one part, where would the body be? As it is, there are*

many parts, but one body. The eye cannot say to the hand, "I don't need you!" And the head cannot say to the feet, "I don't need you!" On the contrary, those parts of the body that seem to be weaker are indispensable, and the parts that we think are less honorable we treat with special honor. And the parts that are unpresentable are treated with special modesty, while our presentable parts need no special treatment. But God has put the body together, giving greater honor to the parts that lacked it, so that there should be no division in the body, but that its parts should have equal concern for each other. If one part suffers, every part suffers with it; if one part is honored, every part rejoices with it..."

When the all-star NBA basketball player **Paul George** was seriously injured a few years ago, his career was declared over. Most of his teammates and opponents and general friends and the public sent encouraging messages and wished him well and hoped he returned to the court. Paul was injured on one leg, so why shouldn't he just go back, hop on one leg, and continue to play as well as he played? Why did the other body parts have to wait on him and one leg to get better before they too could perform to their fullest? By the way, Paul came back and has become better than he was. You don't need to be a genius to answer this. The pain in that leg affected the brain, the other leg, and in fact, the entire body parts had to be there with him to console with him. Not until that leg was healed did the rest of the body parts rejoice and got life back for Paul to do what he does best. Same with most sports players or most career geniuses.

Marc Savard arrived in Boston in 2006 and sprung into his career as a top line center and a top play-maker, averaging nearly ninety points a season between 2005-2009. In 2010, he was blindsided by Pittsburgh player Matt Cook. From this event, he suffered a devastating concussion that was only worsened by a second one in January 2011. These concussions brought Marc's season and career to an end.

How can injury to one single organ of the body take away an entire person's career? The dependency of all other organs to the brain provides us a clear example that systems not seen on the surface must be kept in balance for the entire organism to function.

ONE BODY, MANY PARTS: A METAPHOR FOR LIFE

Toni Conigliaro is the picture of tragic sports injuries. By age twenty-two, the promising Red Sox slugger hit 104 career home runs. However, in 1967, the Boston native caught a pitch just below his eye socket and did not play again until 1969. Though he strove to come back, his vision deteriorated, and Conigliaro was forced to retire in 1971. In 1975, he tried to make another comeback with the Red Sox, but never attained his former glory. After a career wrought with strife, Conigliaro suffered a massive heart attack, and eventually died at just forty-five years of age. However, his legacy still stands within Boston and beyond. Though Conigliaro likely missed out on hundreds of home runs due to his misfortune, he finished his career with 166. In honor of overcoming adversity, the MLB named an award after him. Conigliaro is still seen as a sports icon today.

The human eye should not have been the dictator of such a huge person's career, but it was. If you don't see properly, how do you run, how do you reach and catch balls?

Just consider so many other examples like Muhammad Ali and many others whose careers had to end, either by old age, sickness, or because of an injury to one part of their body.

The above are just a few examples to show how we all need each other in the form of synergy and commonality to succeed. You may get to a bridge only to realize it is too late; you needed that person in order to cross that bridge. Don't make decisions that will affect you negatively. Don't be too quick to say no to unknown opportunities. Don't be too proud to associate with everyone. Don't be too selective in life. If you had the power, you would have selected your own destiny, your family, and where you should come from, the continent to hail from and the parents to have. Have fun in life with everyone.

FOOD FOR THOUGHT:

Respect everyone and learn to work with everyone. Just like the body parts, we all need each other, and we don't need to look the same or be doing the same things to understand that. Businessmen are always on the road traveling, flying in and out, and having big dinners to move on. Without drivers, pilots, and chefs, how could they focus and do well in their business dealings?

SYNERGY AND COMMONALITY

It is only in diversity that we can achieve the best. Diversity in the way we think, the way we look, diversity in our careers, in our special and unique cultures, and everything and everywhere we find ourselves. Embrace unity through diversity and respect each other's viewpoint. However, it's only wise and best to bring everyone together through diversity in every field of expertise to succeed.

✶　✶　✶

CHAPTER 28

The Dangers of Ignoring Cultural Differences

First impressions count when attempting to enter a new market. In order to succeed in the global market, you cannot ignore cultural expectations and expect to increase market share. Guinness in their wisdom has a different taste in different countries. They took time to research what each continent expects in an alcoholic drink. The taste in Africa is much more bitter than it is in Europe because of their different expectations.

You must embrace the notion of understanding and respecting local sensitivities if you desire to succeed. Consider the automaker Chevrolet, whose brand "Nova" sold poorly and failed in Spanish-speaking countries because its name translates as "doesn't go" in Spanish. This might be one of the fastest cars made at the time, but because the name contradicted what it was made to do, it failed. Names count in different cultures and must be watched.

When Proctor & Gamble first released its laundry detergent Cheer to Japan, according to research, it was marketed as an all-temperature detergent, something that was very popular in the United States at the time. What the brand failed to take into account was that the Japanese typically preferred washing their clothes in cold water or tepid bath water; therefore, the all-temperature distinction meant little to them. Later, when the country's cultural norms were factored and marketed properly, its new detergent, Ariel, laid emphasis on how well the product worked in cold water. As a result, Ariel was accepted and was successful, eventually claiming the number three market position at the time.

Showing the sole of your shoes or feet in Iraq is regarded an insult in that culture. It was recorded that former U.S. Congressman Bill Richardson learned that lesson the hard way on a delicate diplomatic mission to Iraq in 1995 under Bill Clinton's presidency. As usual, Richardson crossed his leg while talking to Saddam Hussein at the time, which offended the Iraqi leader, and so he walked out of the room. I believe the entourage may have not initially known why Saddam left the room amidst serious discussions and negotiations, but it was later revealed. That particular mistake might have cost US taxpayers a lot, as the talk was not as fruitful as it was meant to be, but the key takeaway is that they should have studied the Iraqi culture prior to visiting. You cannot visit the Queen of England without having been educated on a few points of etiquette.

Imagine you are in a Vietnamese airport, and, hoping that you can get a seat just on standby, then you cross your fingers for the usual good luck sign. Don't be surprised if people start staring at you. Reason is, in that culture, crossing one's fingers is considered vulgar, as it's said to resemble a certain female's body part.

The 'peace sign' that may mean the same in the US and most part of the world, may not mean the same in other countries, such as Australia, or New Zealand. The indigenous from these countries regard it as an obscene gesture.

Touching of people's heads in certain cultures is a taboo. This is most common in countries with a high population of Buddhists, such as Sri Lanka, Nepal, Thailand, and China. Therefore, if you see a cute kid in any of these countries and pat the child on the head in admiration, like we do here in the US, you would have committed what is regarded as forbidden.

Buddhists consider the head a sacred part of the body. It's where they believe the spirit lives. So, hands off the heads of people in these countries. It is probably just not a good idea to walk around touching stranger's heads no matter which country you are.

Consider this contrast: the red color symbolizes good luck in some countries and that same red color may mean bad luck in another. Red is traditionally a symbolic color of sadness in most Africa countries as an example, unless used on Valentines Days, whereas a country like China, because the names of the dead were previously written in red, it may be considered offensive to use red ink for Chinese names in contexts other than official seals and other happy related issues.

Doing your homework and respecting other cultures is just a great way to start a relationship, or at best avoid having issues. People can end up in jail just because of misrepresentation of a common issue that needed clarity. Others lose businesses because of the simple act of conducting a little bit of research into that culture, or merely overlooking that aspect. Even if the product you offer is superior, affordable, and valuable, people in other cultures won't necessarily be impressed. You must consider what impact local, ethnic and religious beliefs, and values will have on the demand for your product. As well as how your strategies will affect different market structures, according to research and adding common sense.

The use of first names in certain cultures is considered rude while it is welcome in others. Hugging in certain cultures is welcome and regarded normal, while it is frowned upon in others. Shaking of hands is acceptable in one but not in another. We live in a diverse world, and even though we cannot satisfy every culture and everyone, one must make the effort to be seen as trying if we want to live in harmony and in peace.

Advice:

While others attempt to relate and learn your culture, do not expect them to do everything right. There is the need to shift some of your stances and be receptive and appreciative of the effort.

I was invited to give a speech in a particular country. I was aware of the sensitivity of the cultural norms and so, knowing I wasn't perfect but would try everything possible to adhere and respect their culture, I did something unique. Before my speech, respectfully pre-warned the audience that, I would do everything possible to honor their culture, however, in case I did or say anything that didn't fit properly, I should be forgiven! They all laughed and it was happily accepted. During the speech, I found my hands in my pocket briefly as I was conscious of it already. I was surprised when I was done with my most piercing speech, someone whom I respected a lot and who has traveled a lot and was well exposed to other cultures, sitting at the front of the pack came to me and said I shouldn't have put my hands in my pocket. I was happy with the caution but he came across been offended, despite my caution.

FOOD FOR THOUGHT:

I learned that, despite people claiming to accept your mishaps, they sometimes only mean it when you don't falter. Let us learn to accept each other as much as we can and understand that we all cannot be the same or do the same things correctly. Most especially when others try their best to respect yours in a short amount of time. This is diversity too.

※ ※ ※

CHAPTER 29

Different Types of Relationships

There are several types of relationships. Most have already been identified, but take a look at this selection.

1. **Forced relationships:** This is also called, 'Acquired relationships', which include your direct families members, siblings, parents, and the like. These types of relationships are stuck with you for the rest of your life, whether you like it or not, whether you love them or not, whether you care for them or not, or whether you appreciate them or not. You are glued to this mainly by virtue of blood relations.

2. **Purposeful relationships:** These are the relationships that you create purposefully to meet your needs. Usually, you create these types of relationships along your path of life. It could be one of your best friends from college, someone who is intelligent, and so you bonded with him or her, a mentor, a mentee, or any type of comrade that is not forced on you.

3. **Accidental relationships:** These relationships are comprised of coworkers, colleagues, bosses, and the like. With these types, you were not part of the selection as you meet them by virtue of what you do in terms of work, volunteering events, board memberships, or any place where you make a living.

We have friends or just people in general who may help you, hurt you, or don't care about you in any way. They are indifferent as to whether you succeed or not. They just don't care; they stay where they are. The integrity of any friendship or relationship solely depends on you; its success is in your hands. If you hang around seven negative people, you become number eight. Choose your associations wisely, especially in these times.

There are vultures in human beings, and there are squirrels too. There are eagles and lions. If you're in the vulture or squirrel group, you are a destroyer and someone who takes advantage of other people's vulnerability. Be careful of groups like that. If you fall into the lion or the eagle group, you are regarded as courageous, successful, and a go-getter, meaning you will soar up high with confidence and will be able to attack any opportunity as it presents itself. I've always liked the animal kingdom and National Geographic programs, especially when I was much younger. I like the way the cheetah, though regarded one of the fastest animals on land, when it sees a prey, it doesn't just start chasing it simply because it is fast. It strategizes, moves slowly, carefully, gets closer, and calculates its steps. It only raises its head in the bushes when necessary until it gets close enough to start its move. Although it is the fastest animal on land, it also has a weakness. It has a certain mileage it can go at a time, so it usually conserves its energy so as not to waste it. So, in that case, the cheetah speeds up and chases the prey until it could pounce and grip the prey and immediately tackles its neck. This is strategy. The fact that you are liked, you are regarded as intelligent, or because you are in your element today should not give you the opportunity to bluff anyone, rather accept it with humility. Always think and plan ahead. Make the right moves in every aspect of your life, and this obviously includes the choice of relationships. Have you asked yourself why the enormous elephants or hippos, which are much bigger than many other animals, are not regarded the king of the forest? The lion is. Why? Because the lion is a determined animal, rarely scared and daring. It is ready to attack any animal regardless of its size, height, shape, and group they belong to. They are cautious though. They will never attack in the middle of a flock or herds together, but will target only one in particular among the lot. That is the beautiful aspect that intrigues me. They could chase a particular prey among the lot, even if it means bypassing the flock. It will focus solely on the particular one that it wants and not lose focus until it catches it. What is the takeaway? Strategy in attracting or being attracted to the right people is all you need. Learn from the cheetah or the lion, my friend.

Caution:

Do not build your relationship on emotion because emotions will always fade away. Use your mind and heart. Sometimes we spend too much time on good people instead of great people. I would rather lose a good friend to a great one.

FOOD FOR THOUGHT:

The right people are contagious, so in order for someone to succeed in anything they do, one has to, surrounding oneself with the right people and this cannot be overemphasized. Connect with people who are willing to be honest with you, even when it's not something you want to hear, who will support you and alert you when you're on the wrong path, and will be eager to praise you when it's deserved. You need to be receptive in order to be innovative and create new ideas. Learn to be a *"can do"* person or roll with people who are ready to go the extra mile to get things done. By so doing, you are building a strong sense of belonging. Do not mistake commonality and or synergy to mean doing the same thing with the same people all the time. Do not mistake commonality to mean you need to be in the same industry to connect. In fact, commonality in this sense is to connect with people who are doing something different from what you know, learn from them, let them learn from you, and find common grounds on which both of you (or the group) can build a foundation.

I know what my friends do professionally but do not necessarily know what many of them do on a daily basis. I have buddies in the crypto-currency world, and I have friends who are doctors, lawyers, financiers, bankers, politicians, educators, wall street gurus, teachers, faith-based leaders, ordinary people and so on. Though some of them are not directly correlated to my field of work, we found a common ground and are well connected and still remain great buddies. In the same way, you can be in the same field in terms of career with people, share the same type of food, skin color, age, and/or education, but not share the same mindset. Commonality and or synergy, though it can and should be built, is also a kind of spiritual connection with someone. The societies we live in, especially in the western part of the world, do not allow people to care much about another person's lifestyle. It is seen as being nosy. I lived on a beautiful street in one of the states in America for a time, and except for one next-door neighbor, almost no one on the street speaks to anyone. We say hello and wave sometimes, but nothing else. This surprised me. Simply put, what if something is happening to someone for whom all they need is a neighbor picking the phone to call the emergency unit?

A close friend of mine commuted from New Jersey to New York every day on the Path. One day on the train, he was not feeling well. His face was flushed. Most people didn't notice and those who noticed just watched. He needed fresh air so he moved closer to the train doors. As soon as he arrived at the World Trade Center Station, he got out and found a corner to sit down. Everyone on the train went their way, two officers walked right by him. My friend said this was the moment he learned how you could be among millions of people and yet feel so alone. We must put more effort into being a community.

We all need each other one-way or the other. It doesn't matter what political party you belong to, what you eat, or how you dress, treating people with dignity is key.

CHAPTER 30

Followers

A lot of leaders or celebrities have huge number of followers, depending on the size of influence they have, the organization they manage, likeability in society, and many other factors. The funny aspect however is, they only look at their followers from one angle—because they are behind them, it must mean they are leading. As indicated earlier, people may be behind and following you all-right, but what if they are chasing after you, not following as you thought? This is metaphoric, in that, If they are chasing you, this could be dangerous, as they may mean harm to you through blindside. There are people who may pretend to like you but have their secret plans quietly waiting to jump on you when the right time comes to them. Unfortunately, most times they only succeed in the short term. Over the years of my leadership experience, I have come to understand this much clearly, and it is imperative to note that leadership is not always or necessarily to be in the front, but you can strategize where you place the weaker ones in front, then you follow to make sure no one is left behind. Those you think are following you, be careful because when you turn to see them, they might not be there as you think. They are gone because you weren't paying attention to their needs; you were focused on your own self. How do you drive a car without observing all the side mirrors and the rearview mirrors for blind spots? It is good to know also that, there are unscrupulous people who create the blind spot for you to fail too. Be on the alert and don't confuse the two!

In their book, 'The 33 Strategies of War', Robert Green and Joost Elffers described a scenario when they said, because we are always prepared for peace, we are never ready for confrontation, and so we always assume the best. They went on further to say that the world has become increasingly competitive and nasty, be it in politics, business, or arts. We face opponents who will do almost anything to gain an edge. More troubling and complex, they cited, the battles we face mostly are with those who are supposed to be on our side. There are those who outwardly play the team game, who act very friendly and agreeable, but who sabotage us behind the scenes and use the group to promote their own agenda. According to Robert Green and Joost Elffers, others are more difficult to spot, play subtle games of passive aggression, offer help that never comes, and instill guilt as a secret weapon. On the surface, according to them, everything seems peaceful enough, but just below, it is every man and woman for him or herself, this dynamic even relates close families and relationships.

Sometimes you feel you have a connection with a group, but trust me, it's just for a while before you know it was just linked to the job, the environment, the opportunities they desire from you, and when those things are gone and they are no more, you cease to exist, at least in their minds. Do not fool yourself. Build positive and forward-looking relationships. Test those relationships and see the reaction. Sometimes people are together and doing okay until something happens, and immediately their true nature reveals itself. It may be too late at the time, so the need to prune rough hedges along the journey before the destination is crucial.

In his book, 'It Worked for Me' - in Life and Leadership, retired General Colin Powell made it clear that the challenge in public life is to keep your balance. *"Most people are decent and want to reach out to you in kindness. Be pleasant to everyone who is pleasant and civil to you. Ignore the pets, hangers-on, and parasites."* He continued, *"Always remember that celebrity is bestowed on you by the public; use the influence it gives you for worthwhile purposes and not just to pump up your ego. In other words, use your position for good, but don't let it go to your head. Don't believe all you hear or read about yourself, good or bad. Don't make your public life your full-time occupation, and hide frequently from the madding crowd,"* he concluded.

How much truer could this be? This is a book he personally autographed and gave to me for leadership. I had the opportunity to meet him personally the first time during an event that was organized by George De Lama, the President of the Eisenhower Fellowship, during the first-ever all-African global leadership Eisenhower fellowship's final weeks. Together with two other personalities, we were specially invited to meet and have a personal discussion with the General (Rtd) prior to a major keynote speech he gave to the group in New York's City College in 2016. Because it was a personal book given to me, I took time to read every word therein and search for its meaning on the deepest level. This icon is one person I respected from a distance for years, and seeing him personally recognize me for my leadership left me speechless. I use this platform to share this award with my committed committee members who dedicated their careers, time, expertise, finances, knowledge, and wisdom to support the initiative. The irony though was that, in return, I was selected to present an achievement award to General Powell as the outgoing Trustee Chair in June 2018 at Philadelphia in the presence of over four hundred invited dignitaries across the globe. It was an opportunity to share the same platform in-person with the General and via video conferencing with former US Presidents, Secretaries of State, high powered influential leaders, Kings and Queens from other nations and ordinary people, in a nonpolitical environment, with one hundred percent focus on social impact.

One other key message I took away from the General's book was that leaders often refuse to let go of power, especially in the offices they hold. When they do finally, it is important to understand it is over and they shouldn't pretend to be present and chipping in with advice unless needed. He had that relationship with his successor as US Secretary of State, Condoleezza Rice, and although they were close, he did all he could to stay away from shadowing her unless she needed. *"It's over. You had your turn at bat"*. He continued, *"Be gone! Get off the train before somebody throws you off"*. Then he sealed it by saying, *"Spend a moment watching the old train disappear, and then start a new journey on a new train."* I loved this assertion, and it made so much sense to me when I read it. A lot of leaders don't know how to let go and get off the train. Even when they leave, they act as though they are still needed. They are distractions in disguise. Your time has passed. Accept it and move on. The timing was so good to me that I couldn't have asked for anything better than this. Another section of his book makes it clear to not think you're the type of leader who turns on the sun every morning. You're only playing your part at a season in time. Remember, without you, life will still go on. If you are lucky and receive a better opportunity at another company, someone may remember you and say you were a good person, but guess what? While that statement is being said, life will still be going on. Business will go on perfectly without you. Money is still being deposited in the bank. Reports are being created. Lunch is being served and eaten. Stop fooling yourself to thinking life is blurred without you. Play your part and go!

While I admire people, I do not necessarily follow them in terms of how they act per se. I am not the type who easily makes friends. I know a lot of readers who know me will shake their heads in disbelief, but it's true. I like to think I am a nice person by nature and try to make people around me feel comfortable. I always have the principle that you should love everyone but trust few. Maintain relationships in a positive manner, but keep a respectful distance. Or avoid areas of hypocrisy and have a conversation with each other for mutual understanding. Agree to separate or stay.

Speaking of relationships, there was an interesting story about "The Two Ministers": Two different ministers were interviewed to take over a huge religious institution after the retirement of the old one. The first leader came and immediately realized that where the pulpit was placed wasn't at the right position, the way he wanted it. It was in the corner of the chapel and very unpleasant. He immediately ordered the pulpit to be shifted to the middle where he preferred it. He didn't last. When the second leader was invited to take over, however, he too realized the position of the pulpit wasn't right, but instead of shifting it one day, he insisted it be shifted gradually by an inch every week. The congregants didn't notice the change, and before they realized, it was in the middle and everyone was fine with its new location. The second leader obviously stayed longer and was loved. He was successful in many duties due to his collaborative leadership style.

People in search of popularity, self, and or the fact that they see themselves as better than everyone else may do anything possible to hide behind the moon to avoid the obvious. I am not here to lecture you on what is good or bad but to state the reality so that you can make your own choice. Do not be surprised to see this happen to you. As you smile towards such people in an attempt to connect, you may receive a polite hello, and that may be it. Don't expect anything more. This happens mostly in business conferences, and places you least expect. Professional politeness should not be misconstrued as 'invitation to treat'. Once you have knowledge, you will not be taken aback. Some, especially from other parts of the world who come to the western world for greener pastures, spend a considerable amount of time gossiping about each other rather than sharing ideas for success and learning to live together. For those who seem to be surging and succeeding, some of them do not see why they should be nice to another person who rather looks like them. They will prefer to *"show off"* and act in a way that is snobbish to gain respect. Respect? This is absurd! Yes, I agree, some of the people, instead of spending quality time to learn, grow, and associate with people who can help them, spend that same time on negative things that appear positive to them. No matter what you say to help make them change from what they presume to know, some of them just can't get it. They are thinking of instant gratification and what would satisfy them today. People in this category should be avoided and be loved from a distance if you can. They see only what they want to see and refuse to see what they don't want to see or what is in front of them. They will pull you down without you knowing. By the way, most of them are not bad people and may not mean harm—they are only expressing what they think they know. They are empty barrels that are making empty noises. Follow them and trace their background and you will be surprised what will be revealed. Most of them are empty; they only live to impress themselves thinking they are impressing others. If you don't avoid such people, they will convert you. Before you realize, you are rolling in their ship without knowing it. Create positive association in building good relationships with the right people who can shape your future.

A friend whose car broke down recently, took it to a garage where he thought he would get help because one of the garage workers he spoke to was a guy from his continent. He was fooled. Unfortunately, the cost the guy gave him for repairing the car was so exorbitant that without consulting with another dealer, he knew he'd been bamboozled. It was almost like buying a new car in that case. Even though he could afford it, it was not about the money at that time; it was about integrity and reasonability. He then took the car out, went to another dealer, a place where he didn't know anyone. He was able to pay half the price of what he was getting from the previous garage dealer, people whom he thought he knew. Same item, same quality, same problem. It is pathetic how people manipulate others' ignorance but use a different face to cheat another. Sometimes, they play the *"because of you"* game and cheat you. Meaning, they use the pretense of knowing you and so, give you a cost, which you are made to believe is the best and cannot bargain or look for an alternative. Beware of such dangerous, selfish crooks.

FOOD FOR THOUGHT:

Follow your heart and your instinct in every instance, and you will find the best result.

As a leader, you sometimes cannot expect to get everything done one day, especially when you are working with people who have the spirit of 'habituation'. This happens when people get used to a particular situation, mostly negative, and over time see nothing wrong about it anymore. Sometimes, those same individuals may also complain about a particular need, but never overcome. Persistent use of an old mindset makes it normal. People in this category will resist change. I recall when I was recruited to lead a major NGO institution in a particular continent, one of my duties was to transform the institution from old ways of doing things, which was producing less effective results to a revised one, to be more effective, responsive, competitive and create best practice systems. In fact, that was one of my unwritten mandates. I had a meeting with some of the key stakeholders to share thoughts and survey the need. In the meeting, there was a suggestion to renovate the buildings, buy new and modern equipment and software. One member, whom I respected for years because I knew him, immediately asked what was wrong with what they had. I was stunned but kept my cool because this person happened to be someone I looked up to when I was young, the very person who should see the need but was opposed to it. Unfortunately, he was against it but played it with respect though. My boss at the time was out of the country, and so I mentioned it to him upon return. He gave full blessing for the changes and supported every step. Sometimes, those who will support the vision may not be those that you expect to go against you, but this is also life—it happens. My boss, however, did everything he could to curtail obstructions, but there was a division - two camps emerged throughout the reorganization; one group that supported the change and another that opposed it. The first group understood the vision, or at minimum trusted the end result would be better. The second group, however, thought the old way was better; they thought they were at a peak of creativity and so, wouldn't listen to any innovation. This is expected whenever there's a massive organizational change.

Sometimes, those that you fight for are those who, when they get in the boardrooms, may be part of the group that will fight you back. Get used to it if you haven't experienced it before. It has toughened me, and I loved it. When you are confronted with such situations, find a common ground for discussion and debate. Understand that you are dealing with human beings, so life is not always about winning but rather sometimes compromise. If possible, turn away. Watch that train go with joy.

CHAPTER 31

My Invitation to the Martin Luther King Jr. Celebration By the White House

I couldn't sleep properly the entire night prior due to the anxiety, thinking of the type of dress to wear, the expectation, arranging and preparing every step, business cards, where to put the main one and the extras, how to present it, who were the other guests, and how to handle the entire situation. Ladies and gentlemen reading this, it was my first, and I was then an MBA student who happened to be lucky enough to be invited among a few colleagues. What do you expect?

I was a student leader at the time and so had that unique privilege. A select few students, probably about fifteen, were chosen to be in the group that I was in. We were among just a few student bodies privileged to attend this momentous celebration. The room was packed with dignitaries, diplomats, ambassadors, successful politicians, businessmen—you name it. There were these overdressed business-minded students who were trying to impress but not quite catching up. The bow tie was almost perfect, pants were ironed with precision, and the haircut was superb. I wished there was a way to get there without walking or taking a car to this special occasion just so not to wrinkle my well-ironed suite. I wore the best of the shoee, so polished I could see my reflection. My belt neatly held my pants and my neatly buttoned shirt in place. Nothing could move it out of place. Lips shining (sorry ladies, boys are taking over), cufflinks matched the bow tie. Head to toe, I was the archetype of a well-groomed, well-dressed gentleman. I looked good and, damn it, I knew it!

I met various dignitaries, but two personalities in particular stood out. These personalities were looking constantly in my direction. One of them was a former young and famous congressman (name withheld), and the other was a former ambassador from my native country where I originally come from. I was itching to connect with these two folks, but something in me (probably a little pride or fear) was whispering to me not to. So, I ignored the congressman who was looking at me directly and even came close by, but I finally got the courage to naturally get close to the ambassador, and we shared thoughts. I introduced myself, and he did as well, as most of them were wondering where these young *"successfully-looking"* guys were from. You're right! We weren't lobbyists or senators, nor did we even fall into the group of any of their funders, so who were we? They knew the existing president and his family, and they also knew their vice president and many rich people, so our presence was in dilemma to many. All the same, the ambassador and I exchanged business cards, and I mentioned I was from his native country and pursuing my MBA and was honored to have been specially invited to such an occasion. The ambassador was glad and advised me to make sure to be part of the future leaders in the country and urged me to do well and stay in touch. We stayed partially connected until after almost ten years when we reconnected again. At this time, my experience and position in society had changed, so the interest was extremely different. I added value to myself and was able to speak his language much better. Even the first time we connected, it was purely based on commonality in terms of how we looked and where we met. That was simple. Do not play with the power of commonality; use it effectively. This man accepted my invitation to meet in Washington DC. This wouldn't have been considered in the first place if I didn't add value to myself and seem as a promising gentleman. I would have been a waste of time to him.

FOOD FOR THOUGHT:

Add value to your life. It's as simple as that. By virtue of people's daily lives and how busy everyone is, people lose touch, even when they don't want to. Imagine adding value to yourself so that you are in a circle that allows both of you to meet constantly. It is much easier that way, and it gives you the respect that you deserve.

✶ ✶ ✶

CHAPTER 32

The Fruit of Etiquette and Managing Incidental Situations

The phone rang and a lady with a sweet, soft-spoken, and professional voice picked up. She said hello and mentioned the company name, and in her very polished and polite voice, she asked what she could do to assist me. I returned the favor and was extremely courteous as I narrated my frustration for not receiving the required services as expected from their company. I was (rather strangely) feeling guilty telling my story, not wanting to disappoint such a voice over the phone, but I had to stick to my story and stay focused. The company wasn't a bad company—as a matter of fact, they were great—but they needed a bit of a push to get things done. The lady was extremely helpful and listened to me with full attention. She sounded young but eventually told me she was a single mother. She surprisingly opened up to me over the phone. We went on and on, and the entire discussion regarding what I called for turned into a personal conversation. It wasn't until the end of our conversation that I realized how smartly but genuinely she aligned her personal story with mine to cool me down. She was able to find something with a common ground for us to talk about. We talked about children, spouses, disappointments and the economy. We shared a similar trend of concerns and problems we both faced, even though she was working at a place that provided solutions. We were able to connect so much that if you were listening from afar, you might think I was speaking with someone I already knew well.

SYNERGY AND COMMONALITY

After the end of all the discussions, this lady suggested a much better path for me. She even went the extra mile to extend a huge discount for a certain period for me to maintain the existing fee but enjoy superior service. At the time, I was only paying for a single service per month, but now, with the magic help of this angel lady, with the same fee I would enjoy multiple and extra services in the same month. She and I agreed that she would be calling me personally intermittently to check on the status of the case. What else could I ask for? This is the power of commonality. The power and courage this woman had to defend my case was infectious, impeccable, and admirable. Usually one does not need courage to defend the rich, the powerful, the strong, and the wise in society because they really don't need it; they already have it all. They can buy anything regardless of the price tag on it and will stay above water. They don't have to live by many of the rules in this world; however, the innocent, the vulnerable, and the weak suffer for the most trivial things. There is no equal justice in this world whatsoever. Live your life to fight the cause of others who cannot defend themselves: the destitute, the weak, the vulnerable, and the minorities in society. It relates to anyone who has no power at a point in time to defend him or herself. When you move from one school to another, in the first few days, you're the minority. If you can't understand how things are done, then you will need someone to teach and walk you around that situation—you just fell into the minority club in that instance. Even if you are rich and powerful but find yourself in a precarious situation or unfamiliar territory, you're the minority. You will need to adapt to the situation, share empathy, and relate. Imagine living in another country for a while and then later traveling to another country that is unfamiliar territory from what you know, in terms of lifestyle, food, culture, and behavior, you will need to adapt, learn through observation and experimentation, or need someone to help you navigate through your new environment. In those circumstances, you're a minority since for a few moments, you will have to do things differently and will need help to salvage. There would be less commonality in such an environment for you, unless you learn quickly to adapt.

There are varied ways to be found in the minority club. The point here is how one adapts to the situation and how one is helped to adjust to what makes the difference. This is where we need each other and to accept the fact that, we are all intertwined in this world, and even the diversity we have is for a good reason. One cannot do without the other.

✶ ✶ ✶

CHAPTER 33

How Leaders Find Camaraderie Despite Differences

I used to waste my time siding with leaders when they fought, only to see them later having dinner together, laughing and enjoying life. It was like seeing two kids fighting, and then, in the next second, they are together playing and embracing each other.

It is revealed that at U2 concerts in the early 1990s, a regular part of the show featured criticism of US President George H. Bush Senior. The frontman, Bono, could call the White House in the middle of the concert to try to get a chance to speak to the president. When Bush's son, George W. Bush became the 43rd president in 2001, Bono didn't spare him. 43rd didn't go to war with his critic, Instead, he saw an opportunity to invite him so they could discuss life-threatening issues like the malaria pandemic, the spread of AIDS, and debt relief issues at the time. After the meeting, in 2003, Bush started a program in Africa known as PEPFAR, which fourteen years later is credited with saving over eleven million lives with some support from Bono of course.

Bono in recent times, was in Texas, the home of the Bush's, as part of another U2 tour and paid a visit to his old friend the 43rd and they took a photo together. It is amazing what can be accomplished when mature people find common ground for the good of all.

What if the situation was different? Imagine if George W. Bush had decided to ignore or aggravate Bono for his criticism, flexing his muscles as the president. Innocent lives probably would have been lost. Bush and Bono were instead wise enough to turn the situation into friendship.

SYNERGY AND COMMONALITY

Consider also former US presidents Bill Clinton, Jimmy Carter George H. Bush, Barack Obama and George W. Bush. Even though they disagreed with each other over their policies in the past, and probably even today, on issues of common concern, they are united in the interest and protection of American democracy. Whatever differences that may exist now between President Trump and any of his colleagues, that might vanish once they find common ground. Those presidents connected on issues related to global hunger, poverty, and health issues.

During the funeral of President H. Bush, it was revealed that, when Obama traveled to Texas one time, HW Bush (I believe wheelchair bound) came to the airport to meet him. Asked later about that, he classily said, when the president of the United States visits my home state, I will always be there to greet him. It didn't matter to which political party the existing president belong.

Usually, it has become ironic that whenever former US presidents meet and are on the same airplane together, they connect better. For some reason, there is something about being airborne that connects these ferocious opponents, regardless of their differences. The rhetoric about each other in a negative sense reduces after that. I don't know why they don't use that quite often—it works! Let's get more fuel in the tank and more international issues for them to address.

The Clinton's and the Bush's are closer now than you can imagine because they served and, I think, continue to serve on common goals and global initiatives affecting humanity. One such platform is the Presidential Leadership Forum, where you mostly see both of these great men very closely sharing common thoughts, agreeing on each other's points on the same platform. It is said that George W. Bush referred to Bill Clinton as a *"brother from another mother."* Their relationship has soared so well and is very admirable to watch.

The two, who have become friends in retirement, told the graduation of the inaugural class of the Presidential Leadership Scholars program that, failure is a part of life and to keep their ambitions burning so that they can make a difference.

"The American people expect to see some sharp elbows in a campaign. What really discourages them post-campaign is the inability to govern in a way that is congenial," Bush said.

Clinton noted, *"So much in the media today is this culture of anger and resentment. We have to rise above anger to answers, to rise above resentment to a real response,"* he said.

Bush talked about the need to avoid the trappings of power and create an environment around leadership where *"sycophants are not allowed in,"* adding Clinton told him to use big words. The place went into laughter and almost a non-stop clapping for a while. It was electrifying and fascinating to watch.

The former President Bill Clinton in his joking response replied that, his colleague (referring to George Bush, the 43rd) did not know any big words, except perhaps *"itinerant portrait artist,"* apparently referring to Bush's hobby of painting portraits since retirement.

The Presidential Leadership Scholars program is a partnership among the Bush, Clinton, Lyndon Johnson, and George H.W. Bush presidential centers, and it is nice to see these giants get together for a common cause.

It is not too surprising that these two giants connected after retirement, which a magician may not have seen coming. What is more surprising is the level of genuine off-camera friendship that they have. They now consult with each other beyond issues affecting the globe and that of their country, and on personal issues as well. This is why when you are supporting politicians, remember they are and would be friends one day, so try not to be an outlier. Else, you will look like someone gossiping about two lovers who have issues, and you play one side. When they come together, they would discuss you in their private and you may be described as the intruder.

Do you recall the famous 'yelling' of Barack Obama to Bill Clinton in Jerusalem? Let me remind you: *"Bill, let's go. Bill, Bill, Bill—let's go home…"* It was fascinating to watch. This almost the last few months left on Obama's term as US President and they had to attend the funeral of former Israeli President Shimon Peres in Jerusalem and were about to fly back to the US. What an incredible scene to watch, and to see what good friends they have become, so much, that their relationship became infectious. What friendly frustration and laughter. Obama was already aboard Air Force One, and it usually doesn't happen that a sitting president would wait for a former president on a plane—it's always and usually the opposite. Obama was patiently waiting for Bill to board the flight so they could start their long journey home. Bill, as I understand, enjoys pleasantries, so he was spending more time on the tarmac talking with people. After all, Chelsea, his only child and daughter is married and busy, and his wife was busy campaigning at the time, so why rush to get back home? - My funny thought. Obama, on the other hand, had his two young and growing daughters, a wife who wasn't running for any race, and a dog to catch up with. He also happened to have a country to run! Obama might have concluded that if he continued waiting on the airplane, it could take another half an hour to leave. This could only happen when there is friendship and the fact that all the insinuations and rivalry between them when Bill Clinton was campaigning for his wife Hillary against Obama, meant less to them now than their forward-looking relationship, common interest, and trust. They now could see eye to eye.

In their collection and write-up, Nancy Gibbs and Michael Duffy narrated how Obama and Bush shared a ride on *Air Force One:*

State funerals allow presidential adversaries the opportunity to mend wounds and start new friendships. Funerals of historic magnitude can cause those who make history themselves to stop and inwardly focus their attention on their own deaths. While writing eulogies for fellow titans, they cannot help but to imagine their own as they review their personal challenges, hype their accomplishments, and hide their regrets. This time of pause can provide an opportunity to forgive.

When Egyptian President Anwar Sadat was assassinated in 1981, the United States Secret Service decided that it was too dangerous for the then existing president and his vice president to risk attending the funeral, due to high political tensions. Upon deliberation, former Presidents Gerald Ford, Jimmy Carter and Richard Nixon were delegated to attend. During the long flight to Egypt in the Middle East, none of them cared for the other particularly, as they still had their differences and holding onto their ego's. Just after the funeral, Nixon had to steer off to another important commitment, leaving the other former Presidents by themselves. On their return flight back to the United States, Jimmy Carter and Gerald Ford automatically dropped their half-decade of resentment to each other, and realized that they had more in common than either one of them could have imagined. At least, they knew they both dreaded twenty-five years of unexpected retirement, they both despised raising funds in any form, and last but not the least, they both never liked the existing President, Reagan. As humorous as that may be, it also serves as a point of commonality that they shared. This flight was the start to a beautiful relationship that they never had. Over the next two plus decades, the two men joined forces on many projects on social impact. They became great friends, even promising to provide the eulogy for the other when the time came. That honor came to Carter when Ford died in late 2006 and he honored the promise. They both owe it to Anwar Sadat and the long flight.

In November 1963 former Presidents Harry Truman and Dwight Eisenhower, bitter enemies for more than a decade, shared a limo returning from the Arlington Cemetery after the burial of President John F. Kennedy. This quiet ride provided an opportunity for the two men to talk, set their animosities aside, forgive, and mend their old wounds. As the limo pulled up to the Blair House in the darkening Washington twilight, Truman asked Ike to join him inside for a drink. All of the years of difficulty and pain melted away as the hours ticked by and the cocktails were refilled.

In April 2005, President George W. Bush invited his father and Bill Clinton to fly to Rome together to attend the funeral of Pope John Paul II. Clinton knew the senior Bush well, but it was only on this flight that he and Bush really got to know each other. They had many conversations both on the flight and at the American Embassy in Rome. Afterward, Clinton told his aides how much he enjoyed this time. The two men briefly became unlikely part-time business partners, and gave speeches together on many occasions.

During the 2008 US presidential campaign, former Presidents Barack Obama and George W. Bush were not close to one another. Obama blamed Bush for many things. On the other hand, Bush remained publically silent about his thoughts towards Obama saying, "he deserves my silence". However, after Obama's election, the two men formed a friendship bond. The number of times Obama since showered praises on George W. Bush was arguably more than the times he criticized him.

The two former Presidents flew together aboard Air Force One from Washington to Johannesburg to attend the funeral of Nelson Mandela. According to Reuters.com, Obama and his wife Michelle, George W. and his wife Laura, and Obama's then Secretary of State Hillary Clinton flew together aboard Air Force One for the cross-Atlantic trip. The fact that leaders from both parties joined together for Nelson Mandela's funeral underscored the importance of Mandela's life and legacy, said Martha Joynt Kumar, a political scientist at Towson University in Maryland who studies the presidency. In Kumar's words, "it puts a stamp on the importance that the United States' thought of Mandela, his importance as a world leader".

Some say that the longer a person sits in the big chair the more regard he tends to have for all of his predecessors regardless of a country. And, as the stories above illustrate, state funerals provide the chance to heal old wounds, start new friendships and partnerships, and reflect on one's own life.

FOOD FOR THOUGHT:

What binds us together is far more than what divides us. Watch your eyes in heated moments because the eyes you pluck may be the very eyes you may need to guide you tomorrow. The legs you break may be the legs you may need to lead you tomorrow. The hands you damage may be the hands you may need to help you reach something tomorrow. The mouth you slap may be the mouth and the lips you need tomorrow to speak wisdom on your behalf. Politics or corporate life, personal or group, be mindful of your perception about someone when you don't have all the facts. Be careful what you say about someone because you don't know what that person may be for you, or for your generation sometime. We will always have our differences, but we should not let such differences become weapons in our hands. Let's find the commonality and the synergies in us sooner rather than later.

CHAPTER 34

Recipe for a Perfect Taste

You don't need to like everything about someone to have a common ground with that person. That will be impossible in most circumstances. If you spend your time finding what is not in common, you will easily find a lot. The Internet as we know it reflects what you're looking for like a mirror. You cannot dress like a masquerader and expect to see someone in suit and tie through the mirror. I urge you to see the positive more than the negative in people. There is a reason why the piano has two different colors of keys. The white keys produce natural sounds that are naturally more appealing to the ears, whereas the black keys create more dissonant sounds that are less pleasing. They both need each other to create harmony and a fuller sound. It wasn't a mistake when the old-timers made it that way. Simply put, we need each other to forge ahead and succeed. Not until recently did I learn that many inventions emanated from people of color in addition to all the inventions created by white men and women. Let's look at a few of these inventions.

Did you know that it was Sarah Boone, a black woman, who invented and received patent rights for the improvement of the ironing board? Did you know that Jan Ernst Matzeliger, whose mother was of African descent, was a revolutionary in the shoe industry and invented lasting machines that revolutionized the way shoes are made? What about the hair comb? It was Walter Sammons who in 1920 received the patent for the invention and improved comb that straightened hair. Lydia D. Newman, however, invented the hairbrush that could be taken apart easily for easy cleaning and maintenance in 1898. Wow! Did you also know that it was Lloyd Ray who improved and invented the dustpan? They were all black people.

At this point during my research, the number of inventions by blacks stunned me. Let's continue. George T. Sampson invented and got the patent for the automatic clothes dryer in 1892. It was John Lee Love, a carpenter, who invented the portable pencil sharpener known as Love Sharpener.

At this point, I began to wonder why we couldn't all live together in harmony. But we aren't done yet. William Purvis invented the first fountain pen, bag machines, a bag fastener, a hand stamp, an electric railway device, an electric railway switch, and a magnetic car-balancing device. And John Albert Burr invented one of the first rotary blade lawnmowers.

"Each man is an island unto himself. But though a sea of difference may divide us, an entire world of commonality lies beneath."

- James Rozoff

Robert Bowie Spikes invented the automatic gear shift device based on automatic transmission for automobiles, as well as the beer tap, automobile directional signals, and a safety braking system for trucks and buses. George Carruthers built the first telescope at age ten and has spent his life making important contributions to the study of outer space.

It was Joseph Gammel who invented the supercharger for internal combustion engines. Garret Augustus Morgan experimented with a liquid that gave sewing machine needles a high polish that prevented the needle from scorching fabric as it sewed. In 1905, he accidentally discovered that same liquid could also straighten hair. He invented the black hair oil dye and invented a curved toothcomb for straightening in 1910. He also invented the safety hood smoke protection device after seeing fire fighters struggling from the smoke they encountered in the line of duty. His device used a wet sponge to filter out smoke and cool the air - this was the predecessor to the gas mask. He was also granted the patent, with his colleagues for traffic control device that had a third warning, which he later sold to General Electric in the mid 1920's. If it were not for Elbert R. Robinson, there would not be electric buses today because he invented the first electric trolley and patent for improving the railway system, which had been improved over time.

Thomas Elkin vastly improved the refrigerator. And it was Alive H. Parker who first invented the gas-heating furnace that gives heat to us today. What about the cooling system? Frederick Jones first invented the cooling refrigerators to sustain perishable goods for easy and longer transportation to needed areas.

I was even more puzzled to note Lewis Howard Latimer invented the electric lamp. Charles R. Drew, a black scientist, invented the best possible ways to successfully store any kind of blood for future analysis leading to blood bank technology. Dr. Daniel Williams was the first black who performed the world's first successful open-heart surgeries, while Phillip B. Downing invented the first open letter mail drop box. William Barry invented the mail distributing and stamp-canceling machine, and Alexander Mills invented the first automatically opening and closing elevator.

FOOD FOR THOUGHT:

We need to find the areas that connect us as human beings rather than areas that do not. Black history is far more than black slavery, suffering, captivity, torturing, freedom fighting, and so on. It is also about inventions, legacies, and the positive mark they too had and continue to create in the world in spite of the limited chance they had at the time—and, arguably, to date. The lesson to take away is that we all need each other at all times. Imagine me starting to mention the invention of the white. It will be another book in itself, but the point is how we complement each other more than we know. White, black, 'blue', 'red', 'green' or what have you, we can do less without each other, since all are uniquely gifted to complete the life's puzzle.

SYNERGY AND COMMONALITY

"If you ask what the people here are like, I must tell you, 'Like people everywhere!' Uniformity marks the human race."

- Johann Wolfgang von Goethe, The Sorrows of Young Werther

✶ ✶ ✶

CHAPTER 35

Friends, Foes, History, and Commonality

One of my favorite books that still inspires me today (in fact, I have read it more than six times and watched the movie a few times), is a book authored by Jeffrey Archer called 'Kane and Abel'. The story takes you on dramatic trails and scenes where two boys were born on the same day but from different family structures and in different continents. Kane was born in a wealthy family in America, spoon-fed and pampered. He attended the best schools, including Harvard, and became one of the richest and best bankers who ever lived. Abel, on the other hand, who was born as Wladek and later changed his name to Abel, came from one of the poorest families in Poland. In fact, he was adopted while his mother delivered him in the wilderness - she died in childbirth. Abel had to be re-adopted into a rich Baron's castle because he was intelligent and the Baron wanted a challenge for the son. After a few years of glory in the castle, they were captured and became prisoners of war, and then his life turned sour. He had to go through the toughest life moments, after his village was invaded, everyone taken captive and later both the Baron and his only son died, or killed. Before the Baron's death, on his dying bed, he called on Wladek and a few others to witness his sole decision to give Wladek the Baron's band, indicating, he would inherit him. He suffered from the price of war and was later taken to America, which was when he changed his name from Wladek to Abel. He built his life as a waiter and continued into hotel management, and over time he became as rich as Kane. Even though their paths crossed through the coincidental marriage of their children, one thing they had in common, they both detested each other, especially Abel. Abel's hatred for Kane was unbearable, thinking it was Kane who caused the death of his best friend, Davis Leroy, and later denied him a loan to rebuild the Richmond Hotels. It was fascinating to note after the death of Kane that, little did Abel know, it was Kane who secretly borrowed the needed amount of two million US dollars ($2 million) through a private firm to help Abel because he saw him as a good investment. William Kane did that to conceal any conflict of interest because he was a banker. In the fine print, it wasn't supposed to be revealed to Abel who the loaner was until the death of one of them, more so if it is Kane first. Just as the fine print stated, the intermediary firm followed the instructions to the very last dot. And so, it was after the death of Kane that Abel learned the truth. He cried and regretted all the years of hatred he had for the very person who rather saved his life. Though Kane knew the source of Abel's wealth, he acted as though he didn't. At the end, their children got married and they took over their wealth and merged it for their grandchild after the death of Abel. They may have been enemies in life, but they became friends in death. Their children's children lived to portray what their parents failed to do.

In that same vein, while Nelson Madiba Mandela was regarded in recent times as one of the first leaders to have brought enemies or counterparts together, by choosing his vice president from the apartheid regime and later adding his second opponent to hold a major ministerial position.

History reveals that John Adams and Thomas Jefferson, former American presidents did something similar in an intriguing way.

Although John Adams and Thomas Jefferson had known each other in Congress even before America had its first president, they both had different opinions on what leadership meant. They both had one goal and commonality, and that was liberating their country (in those days, called the colonies). In addition, they were equal intellectuals by all standards and were regarded as two of the best in the country. However, they had major differences in how they thought the country should be led. While John Adams believed in very strong central government and its controlled policies, Thomas Jefferson believed the people should have more say in their affairs with less government intervention. Jefferson's argument was, if they allow strong government control, where then lies the difference in what they were fighting for? What would be the difference from what they got from the British? To him, that would mean just changing leadership but literally doing the same thing, and Jefferson didn't see the point in taking that approach. So, these two friends started having issues amongst themselves. Unfortunately for Jefferson, the people at the time ironically loved Adams' idea, and so did George Washington, the first president. Adams was favored and seen as a hero. Adams and Jefferson, however, worked under the first democratically elected president, George Washington, in the same cabinet. Jefferson and Adams had known each since 1776, and later when they traveled to Europe in the same period for a number of years on official assignment, they were in contact with each other.

Jefferson was known as a very intelligent and quiet person, while Adams was the opposite, loud and vociferous. Due to his intellect, Jefferson was the one who was asked by the then leaders in Congress to write the Declaration of Independence for America. It took him less than a week to complete it. I believe his peers believed in him as someone who could do a better job, but little did they know he would write the Declaration in that short amount of time. Without a doubt, that achievement catapulted his recognition amongst his peers.

George Washington picked his vice president to be John Adams, and Jefferson became the first secretary of state. They were all first in their positions.

Jefferson and Adams' differences pushed them mentally away from each other, even though they were physically present at cabinet meetings. It became apparent that Jefferson might have been more isolated due to his belief in leadership, so in 1793 he decided to leave and go back to his farm in Virginia.

Three years after what Jefferson thought to be a political retirement, in 1796, he was on the platform again to campaign against his former friend John Adams after George Washington decided not to run for a third term. We all know how politicians act, mostly when they want to occupy a particular seat in government, what they do on the campaign trail. These two were no different.

John Adams came out as the winner of the presidency, and so became the second president after George Washington. John Adams then did something people never thought of—despite the huge differences between them, he picked Jefferson to be his vice president.

SYNERGY AND COMMONALITY

Once a lion, forever a lion; you cannot change to be an eagle. So even though Adams and Jefferson were the two most powerful leaders, they continued to disagree with each other as far as their ideas to lead the nation were concerned. At this point, Adams was losing popularity, and Jefferson was gaining it as the tables have turn. The very people who wanted the type of government Adams proposed initially, began to turn against him. In the 1800 presidential election, Jefferson again campaigned against his boss and successfully defeated him. This shocked Adams, and naturally he was infuriated by the embarrassing loss.

Just days before Adams left office, he nominated a lot of new Supreme Court Judges who wouldn't favor Jefferson's ideas and his presidency. Since judges could not be fired until they died or something out of the ordinary happens to them, he thought it best to destroy Jefferson's leadership, or at least frustrate him. Jefferson had no choice but to find a common ground to work with these judges and focus on mutual areas of agreement.

Adams and Jefferson's relationship was more as silent enemies at this point, but a common denominator they both had was a man named Benjamin Rush, who was with them from the start in 1776 and happened to have been one of the signatories to the Declaration of Independence. He did everything possible to bridge the differences that had divided them for so many years, but he was unsuccessful. Sometimes, it is good to leave things to nature. Usually, when people grow, they become wiser than you think. So, nature took over, and in a surprising move, Adams took the first step. This was after they both left office. I believe Adams looked back and might have felt sad for how he had treated Jefferson, and so he was humbled enough to send him a book in 1811 while they were both in retirement. I also believe Jefferson was surprised and excited about that step because, deep down, it was not Adams as a person he disliked, but rather his principles. He too might have also wanted peace, but as we know, when egos clash, it is difficult to withstand it. No wonder their common pal Benjamin Rush couldn't bring them together after trying for so many years.

Jefferson, who loved to write, wrote a thank you letter back to Adams. It is interesting to note though that Jefferson and Abigail, Adams' wife, were good friends and continued to write to each other over the years despite the differences between the two 'ego's. That book ignited their friendship again until their death. The sad and magical part of this story was the fact that Jefferson died exactly fifty years after signing the Declaration of Independence. What a coincidence. But a much bigger coincidence was that Adams also died that same day, later in the afternoon. Because messages traveled much more slowly in those times, Adams had no idea that his friend Jefferson had passed. And so, before he finally died, he said, "*Jefferson still lives.*"

What a way to live and die. Indeed, friends, foes, history, and commonality got mixed up. They admired each other, loved each other, hated each other, were both incredibly intelligent, were both part of the Continental Congress, both had parts in writing and approving the *Declaration of Independence*, were both presidents and vice presidents. And despite their differences, they had one major thing in common: they both had great love for their country.

As to the details of their leadership, what they believed in or did does not form part of this story. The focus is how these two leaders found a common place in their hearts to lead and govern.

One piece of advice is upon getting to know the life stories of these great leaders and how they could have done things differently is to understand that - you're allowed to be frustrated and even prepare your message. However, don't press the send button until after a day or two to confirm your intent and anger level. This is because it is almost impossible to retrieve what you have sent, so think well before you act on it.

FOOD FOR THOUGHT:

This goes to show that synergy and commonality could be positive or negative. However, if it is positive, that is what forms the key to success. This is how history describes these political giants as friends, foes, and how they used commonality to overcome their challenges. This also goes to confirm that, what divides us as human beings is less significant versus what brings us together and its effects on society.

FINAL FOOD FOR THOUGHT:

- Character is how you treat people who can't do anything for you, therefore treat people with dignity and respect, you never know, your miracle may be in the hands of an ordinary person.

SYNERGY AND COMMONALITY

- Just as the climbing lianas and the redwood trees rely on one another's support systems to succeed, one cannot do without others.

- Regardless of the color of your skin, where you are born (for which you didn't contribute or have the opportunity to decide), how you were born, or to whom you were born, we are all almost the same in the way we were birthed. In terms of fetus to a human.

- There is time for everything under the sun. Time to be born, time to die. Learn to do the right thing at the right time.

- There is a thread of commonality amongst successful people and what it takes to rise to the top. If you desire to succeed, desire also what it takes to get you there. And when you get there, learn how to sustain that wealth, else it will fly away like a bird.

- Knowing who you are and identifying the type of people you surround yourselves with, has an effect on your life. If you surround yourself with seven negative people, you're number eight.

- It is important to network and know people, but what is most important is who knows you back.

- The tongue is a very small member of the body, but has considerable impact when used correctly or incorrectly. Consider the size of a ship, but it takes only small rudder to steer it, so guard the tongue.

- Excuses are necessary tools for incompetence and failure. If people like Louis Braille and Harriet Tubman among many others, could overcome their nemesis and turn the negative into positive, why complain –why not you?

- Listening is far beyond just hearing. There is a reason why we have two ears and one mouth. Paying attention and not assuming what is being said to you is key.

- Most times, the difference between ignorance and wisdom is knowledge and exposure. Living your life entirely on per-

- ception is recipe for disaster - so do not judge anything by its cover, which applies to people.
- Identifying the similarities or differences in a Mentor and Advisor is key. This book serves as a coach to help determine these fine lines and how to manage both.
- Appreciating the power of synergy and the diversity we have, be it in talents, capabilities, origin, how someone speaks, dresses and or behaves is what makes the world complete. Embracing each other like the metaphor of the different body parts we have and how they play their parts to make us complete is not different from differences in the human race.
- Taking into consideration cultural differences in life and in business are keys to success, ignoring them is disaster. Consider the automaker Chevrolet, whose brand "Nova" sold poorly and failed in Spanish-speaking countries decades ago, because its name translates as *"doesn't go"* in Spanish.
- How leaders and people find camaraderie despite differences they may have. Be it, socially or politically. How occasions like state funerals, sitting on long flights, or sharing the same passion brings people together. It's magical.
- The unwillingness to acknowledge one's mistake is what becomes the deal killer, instead of the deal breaker, rather, it is often the ones that acknowledge it and seek help that gets to the top.
- Do not relent in doing good. Constantly sow in people, though the benefits may not come to you directly, continue to do your part because, in so doing, someone is also being prepared for you.
- Make every experience an education and every education an experience. That's the only way you can replace complaints with appreciating life's gifts.
- Finally, consider how once friends became enemies, then use the power of commonality through a gesture of exchange of letters and a book to become friends again. Ironi-

cally, they both died exactly fifty (50) years on the day of signing the Declaration of Freedom for America in 1776 – these gentlemen were Thomas Jefferson and John Adams. It is therefore clear that, the key to successes in life and beyond is mostly achieved through synergy and commonality, by allowing people a space around you, through diversity, and learning to endure today's short-term pains to enjoy the fruits of your labor in the future.

APPENDIX

The Seven Main Wastes in Business

When I was on the corporate ladder in my previous life, I was eager to make a difference. I therefore taught, coached, and led in these areas to share my little wisdom in all sectors to create a difference. I spent time teaching and demonstrating how to navigate through systems, how to harness the wastes under one lean management, and how to turn them into real return on investment for total turnaround. My goal was to contribute my part as a unit, under the main agenda for synergistic success.

Among many other things, one of my signature and basic coaching in operations management that I drove and still continue to drive is the seven common wastes in production and process management. It is non-linear in nature. It may be simple but easily ignored, where most institutions either have less knowledge on, or knows some part and do not have full direction on how to manage it. This may seem to fit a particular business model, but these wastes could apply to how we live our daily lives as well, which has nothing necessarily to do with manufacturing set-ups nor systems-oriented institutions. Let me use this opportunity to just highlight them on a 10,000 feet level for you below. :

1. **Inappropriate processing:** Not processing things in the right manner, thereby leading to waste. This leads to higher cost of materials and inefficiency in the system, which needs to be managed from the very beginning.

2. **Overproduction:** Not planning well enough towards producing exactly what is needed and ending up overproducing, thereby increasing cost and negating the opportunity to make extra income.
3. **Overstocking:** This is closely related to inventory. This is where you stock more than is needed at a time, thereby taking money from other activities, paying more rent, and taking extra space from other activities.
4. **Defects:** When a company or individual continues to suffer constant flaws instead of trying to get it right the first time, this increases production cost because the process will have to be repeated before getting it right. Note the amount of time, energy, and extra resources that might be needed and taken away from other important activities to correct the damage. This is different from innovation and the amount of time it has to take to get it right. This is like hiring people who are supposedly experts to perform a duty but constantly finding them not getting it right. Because most businesses work like a chain, the process is delayed as the next person has to wait until the correction is done. However, salaries are paid, bonuses are created, and coffees are drunk during office hours at the expense of the company.
5. **Transportation:** This is using the wrong means of movement to deliver a message, a product, and/or an item, which may land at the wrong place. Take, for example, a product needing to arrive in a particular country the following day, yet instead of using, for example, air transport as the quickest means, one relies on sea transport, which may take several days, if not weeks, to arrive. Imagine using the wrong person in the institution to convey a message, which becomes inappropriate and might damage the reputation of the company, especially if that person does not have the expertise to speak on that specific topic. Or imagine delivering a message too soon, thereby creating confusion amongst experts and resultantly disaffecting expected results. Knowing and using the right means of transportation, as we can deduce from the above examples, is about conduit, not necessarily a physical vehicle. A human being also is a vehicle in this case. Proper transportation is vital whatever the vehicle may be.

6. **Excess motion:** While it is important to analyze and produce the best result, over-analysis can produce what is termed *"analysis paralysis."* Analyze but do not paralyze the situation. I know a lot of leaders who by virtue of trying to satisfy everyone, end up delaying progress over an activity that could have taken less than a quarter of the time expended. The consequences include spending years on what should have taken months. By then, the energy and the joy might have left everyone involved. Do it right by doing it with the right measure to get the right result.
7. **Waiting:** The last thing any executive or business owner detests is wasting time by waiting. Unused time is one of the most painful wastes of resources one can consider. Imagine being in a long line of traffic, waiting to get to your destination, yet for hours you experience no movement. Imagine waiting for a product's part to add to another to complete a process, and for weeks, nothing is heard of it. Waiting is a painful exercise for anyone to go through, and it is expensive to fund.

   Upon thorough research and observation, I came across two additional wastes:
8. **Unused talent:** You need to open your eyes to see the many unused talents that exist. Talented people sit next to us every day without us knowing it. Some of the talents may be known all right, but because they are not appreciated, they end up not being used. Also, sometimes, the big mistake of misalignment plagues us— placing the right talent to the wrong tool/job.
9. **Knowing all of the above eight wastes but doing nothing about them:** This last type of waste is the worst of all. Why would one notice any or all of the above but intentionally do nothing about them? Dismiss such a person without any regret. Sometimes we politicize issues. You can like someone, but that does not mean when they do the wrong thing, you applaud them. If this person owns the business, sorry, that business won't last the journey. Get off that seat and let someone manage you.

   The eighth and ninth wastes, as far as I am concerned, are the biggest wastes of all, in terms of process management, operation, manufacturing, and general business management.

* * *

About the Author
- Evans Kwesi Mensah

Evans Kwesi Mensah, also known as 'Selorm' is a happy father of three amazing boys, as well as blessed with a strong and supportive wife whom he describes as his 'boss'. He is also an honoree of the prestigious Washington D.C. 'Made Man' Global Leadership Award for 2018. It is a global multi-tiered institution designed purposely to honor the extraordinary accomplishments of notable influencers for their leadership and lifetime achievement in their respective fields of work, social impact and consciousness, and significant contributions to communities at large.

Evans has over decades of years' experience in business strategy development and consulting globally, specifically in North America, Africa, and Europe. He became an executive leader in various institutions in these continents and held many senior global leadership positions with Fortune 500 companies. Evans is an expert in Strategy Formulation, Supply Chain Management, Executive Instructor, Operations, Public Speaking and is a Lean Six Sigma Black Belt certified. He is known for turning businesses around and heavily involved in supporting project management initiatives for country development through sustainability initiatives. Some of Evans' clients include the World Bank, Mining segments, Educational sectors, Franchise establishments, Faith-based institutions, Governmental agencies, and NGO fields. He is a strategist with a track record in cross-management that includes but is not limited to cross-cultural management, mentoring, marketing, investment, business productivity, and capacity building.

Evans is a National Council Member for the United Nations Association of USA and doubles as chair for the Collaboration and Partnership Committee (SDG 17). He serves on many boards locally and internationally and giving back to many institutions. Some of which include Charter Board Partners for Omar D. Blair and Howard University Executive Education, where he duos as guest lecturer in the capacity of Executive Coach. He is also honored to serve as a mentor for Watson Institute and guest lectures at Metropolitan State University, all in the USA. He is also an invitee to many other universities and schools. As well, he serves as the country chair for the D. Eisenhower Fellowship for Ghana, a prestigious program that exists to inspire leaders around the world by providing unique opportunities to collaborate and learn from like-minded executives across national borders.

Evans started his preliminary education in Ghana, and later earned his honors bachelor's degree from the University of Greenwich, London in the United Kingdom, and Master's in Business Administration from Howard University in Washington DC, United States of America.

His biggest passion is supporting any venture that has social impact effect as his philosophy is changing one life at a time.

More on the author can be found on his personal website on: www.evansmensah.com or his business page on: www.value-cycle.com. Please send all inquiry emails to: info@evansmensah.com.

www.ingramcontent.com/pod-product-compliance
Lightning Source LLC
Chambersburg PA
CBHW060641150426
42811CB00078B/2244/J